Nature Library

TREES

Nature Library

TREES

Keith Rushforth

Optimum Books

Artists

Henry Barnet, Ian Garrard, The Hayward Art Group, Tim Hayward, David More, David Pratt, Karel Tholé, The Tudor Art Agency Ltd., Ross Wardle.

This edition published by Optimum Books 1983
Prepared by
Newnes Books
Astronaut House, Feltham, Middlesex, England
and distributed for them by
The Hamlyn Publishing Group Limited
Rushden, Northants, England.

Copyright © Newnes Books Limited 1983

ISBN 0 600 35622 1

Printed in Italy

Photographic Acknowledgements

AUSTRALIAN INFORMATION SERVICE, LONDON 67; BIOFOTOS, FARNHAM: Heather Angel 26 – 27, 39, 41, 43 bottom, 48, 61, 65; BRUCE COLEMAN, UXBRIDGE: Gene Ahrens 9 top, Eric Crichton 38, Hans Reinhard 6 – 7; FORESTRY COMMISSION, FARNHAM 19 centre, 19 bottom, Dr. Julien Evans 66; HAMLYN GROUP PICTURE LIBRARY 15 top, 15 bottom, 16, 17, 19 top, 21 top, 21 bottom, 22 top, 22 bottom, 29 top, 29 bottom, 32 top, 32 centre, 32 bottom, 76; BRIAN HAWKES, NEWNHAM 36 – 37; NATURAL HISTORY PHOTOGRAPHIC AGENCY, HYTHE 51, 52, 58, J. Bafree 28 bottom, Douglass Baglin 26, Anthony Bannister 27 top, 43 top, N. A. Callow 23 top, J. Cambridge 8 bottom, 70, D. N. Dalton 30 bottom, Stephen Dalton 12, 57 left, Douglas Dickens 28 top, 30 top, 31, Brian Hawkes 96, E. A. Janes 8 top, 14, P. Johnson 73 left, Jerg Kroener, 40, M. Morcombe 25 top, Ivan Polunin 24, 72, 74, M. Williams 75; KEITH RUSHFORTH, WINCHESTER 13, 23 bottom, 57 right, 73 right.

Contents

Preface

If it were not for the spread of the human race there would be vastly more trees and greater areas of forest on the face of the earth, and their appearance would often be entirely different. Mankind has brought about great changes in his environment both by reckless destruction of forests in the pursuit of rapid financial gain, and by significant alteration of forest types. In the context of the geological time-scale it was physical factors – climate, altitude, soil type and so on – that determined whether a region could support a forest of some kind, but man's influence has now made itself felt with relative suddenness and left its mark in every part of the world.

In areas where the equable climate has favoured the development of human civilization, the exploitation of forest resources has caused damage that is irreversible. Much of the Mediterranean region was once covered with broadleaved forests and pines, but these have now all but disappeared and the scrubby maquis that remains is of little use except for its minor role in soil stabilization. Of course people were for a long time ignorant of the long-term effects of felling trees on a large scale, but in the pillaging of the Mediterranean forests there is a lesson for all interested parties to see. Despite this, in some parts of the world forests are continuing to disappear and are not being replaced.

I hope that a wider understanding of trees, and of the role they play in the intricate global web of plant and animal life, will eventually lead to a more restrained and appreciative approach to their felling and use.

K.R.

Introduction

Trees live and trees die. Some of the mysteries of their lives are shared in the following pages, as is the joy of their beauty and their identity. The trees discussed and illustrated are a mere fraction of the world's full range of trees. The choice has been limited to a useful and interesting selection. Common trees of the northern and southern hemispheres, along with important crop trees, are illustrated and discussed.

Trees are very important to our lives and also very beautiful. They provide many services and benefits which other plants or animals are unable to offer: these range from timber products and essential oils, to flavourings and foods and a wide range of amenity benefits. A landscape without trees is an appalling idea to most people, but such landscapes will become increasingly common as man's rapacious appetite for wood and for forest land puts intolerable pressures on the world's remaining forest resource.

All trees have at least one name, the principal one being the botanical name. When botanists began naming trees in a scientific manner in the 1700s, Latin was the one European language understood by all educated people. It was used then to give living organisms their international name, and the system is still in use today. The name is composed of two elements – a genus name and species name. A **genus** (plural **genera**) may be composed of one or more **species**, and whilst many trees from different genera may have the same species name, the combination is always unique. All the species within one genus have several characteristics in common, mainly concerned with flowering and fruiting. The individual members of any species have in common a certain number or arrangement of characters. In *Acer pseudoplatanus*, *Acer* is the genus name and *pseudoplatanus* the specific name. Sometimes a species is further split into two or more smaller units, called **varieties** or **subspecies**. Selected individuals of species or hybrids are propagated by cuttings: they are then

New life beginning and old life ended. The top picture shows Beech seedlings under parent trees; most of them will not survive to become adult trees because little light reaches the forest floor except in early spring, and all green plants need light in order to grow. The lower picture shows the bole of a Beech tree that reached a ripe old age before dying, and now provides a home for Bracket Fungus.

called cultivars or clones. The Latin name usually tells something of the plant – what it is like (*Sequoiadendron giganteum* is very big), where it comes from (*Persea americana*, the Avocado, is native to Central America) or who found it (*Magnolia wilsonii* was first discovered by Ernest Wilson in 1904). The Latin name of a hybrid is given with the species name preceded by a cross, e.g. *Populus* x *canescens*.

Genera which share floral and fruiting characters are placed together into **families**. Most of the two-page sections in the second half of this book are devoted to a single important family.

Common names are convenient and often more easily remembered, but are pertinent to only a local area or dialect and can be very confusing in an international context. The example cited above, *Acer pseudoplatanus*, is called Sycamore in England, Plane in Scotland and Sycamore Maple in America, where the trees called Sycamore is a true Plane (*Platanus occidentalis*).

In other European languages *Acer pseudoplatanus* is called Faux platane or Erable sycomore in French, Berg-Ahorn in German, Gewone esdoorn or bergesdoorn in Dutch, Vuorivaahtera in Finnish and Sicomoro in Spanish. The biblical Sycamore, of course, has nothing to do with this tree – it is a fig, *Ficus sycamorus*.

Trees make a great contribution to the quality of life; this is emphasized by the contrast between the pleasantly wooded farmstead in Vermont, USA, and the treeless dereliction of the industrial landscape shown below, where sulphur dioxide pervades the atmosphere.

How trees grow

How new growth is made

New growth in plants is made from special groups of cells, called **meristems**, occurring mainly at the tips of the shoots. The most conspicuous example of new growth is seen in spring when deciduous trees reclothe themselves with new leaves from meristem tissue, which is protected over winter in the buds. If you cut open a bud, you will find that inside the bud-scales are a number of pre-formed leaves (choose a tree with large buds, such as a Horse Chestnut). When winter ends, these ready-made leaves quickly expand and the tree is soon green and leafy. However, most plants do not make new extension (long) shoots until later – that is, in early summer when the risk of spring frost damage has passed. Extension growth is made when the shoot between the leaves expands, and new leaves and new shoots are made. Only when the shoot is soft and green can it grow longer; once it becomes woody it cannot – in fact it tends to contract slightly. As the days shorten after midsummer, extension growth stops and the buds for the following year's growth are formed.

Below: **a three-year-old Horse Chestnut twig showing winter buds and large leaf-scars, or 'traces'.**

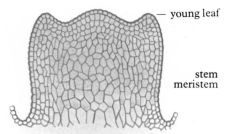

in this region, cells undergo differentiation to form specialized cells

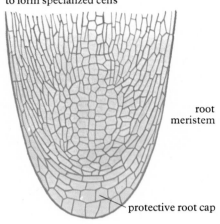

Above: **meristem tissue. Each cell contains the chemical information necessary to develop into any of a range of adult tissues.**

Structure of the stem

The trunk of a tree consists of a number of elements which have special functions, and which can tell us about the tree.

Around the outside is the **bark**, and if you look closely you will see that it consists of two very different parts. The outer layers of the bark consist of dead cork-like cells; these serve to protect the trunk from the outside world. The inner layer consists of living cells, the function of which is to transport the sugars made in the leaves to other parts of the tree.

The central part of the stem is composed of wood. Each year a new layer of wood is formed. In the spring and early summer, the type of wood formed is designed to carry large quantities of water from the roots to the leaves; it is relatively soft, with large water-conducting vessels, and is called **springwood**. Later in the summer, cells with thicker walls are laid down to give the tree support; these cells are called **summerwood** and are darker in colour than the springwood. Spring and summerwood show as alternate bands and by counting these bands you can work out the age of the tree. The live wood around the outside of the tree is called **sapwood** whilst the darker wood in the centre is dead and is called **heartwood**. Heartwood has deposits in it which make it durable.

Growth in the stem only occurs in the cambium, which is a thin layer of cells between the bark and the wood.

Structure of a leaf

The function of leaves is to use energy

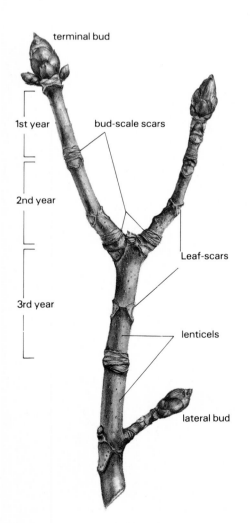

Below: **cross-section of a tree trunk. Each band contains springwood (which is light in colour) and summerwood (dark), and** represents one year in the life of the tree. This tree was about 75 years old.

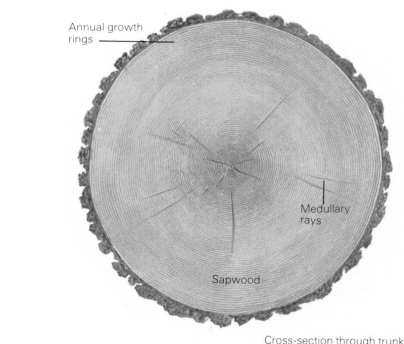

Cross-section through trunk

from the sun to combine water with carbon dioxide from the air to make sugars. Leaves are also designed to distribute the products of this process, which is called **photosynthesis**.

The plant has to control its use of water and the epidermis, the outermost covering of the leaf, is made impermeable, usually by a thick waxy cuticle. Special pores called **stomata** (singular **stoma**) open into the centre of the leaf, so that carbon dioxide can diffuse in and oxygen, which is a by-product, diffuse out. The largest part of the leaf is the green area, which contains the **chloroplasts** where photosynthesis occurs. The veins are the conducting tissue, with wood or xylem cells bringing water and nutrients from the roots and phloem cells, as found in the inner bark, taking the products of photosynthesis around the tree.

Right: **cross-section of a broadleaved tree leaf, such as Sycamore, showing the photosynthetic cells, or chloroplasts, and the midrib and secondary veins.**

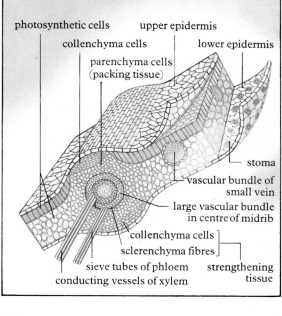

photosynthetic cells   upper epidermis
collenchyma cells   lower epidermis
parenchyma cells (packing tissue)
stoma
vascular bundle of small vein
large vascular bundle in centre of midrib
collenchyma cells
sclerenchyma fibres   strengthening tissue
sieve tubes of phloem
conducting vessels of xylem

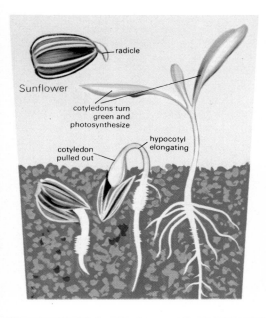

radicle
Sunflower
cotyledons turn green and photosynthesize
cotyledon pulled out
hypocotyl elongating

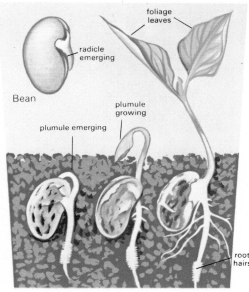

foliage leaves
radicle emerging
Bean
plumule growing
plumule emerging
root hairs

Far left: **hypocotyl germination, in which the seed leaves, or cotyledons, are lifted above the soil.** *Left:* **epicotyl germination – the cotyledons remain below the ground and a shoot or 'plumule' is pushed above it.**

Below: **segment of a stem showing bark, sapwood and heartwood. The cambium which separates the bark and the wood is a thin layer of cells which divide, forming** xylem (wood) cells on the inside and phloem (bark) cells on the outside. The cambium is the only part of the stem in which growth occurs.

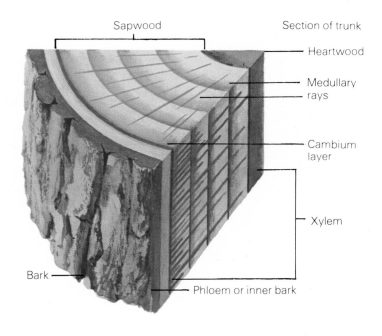

Sapwood   Section of trunk
Heartwood
Medullary rays
Cambium layer
Xylem
Bark
Phloem or inner bark

Germination of seeds

To germinate, a seed must absorb water and expand, breaking the seed coat. It then pushes out a primary root called the **radicle**. This grows down into the soil.

There are then two ways by which germination may be completed. The commonest method is for the radicle to pull the **cotyledons**, or seed leaves, out of the seed coat and raise them above the ground. Photosynthesis then begins and true leaves are made. Sycamore and Ash are examples of common trees using this form of germination.

In the other method the cotyledons remain below ground in the seed coat and a shoot, bearing true leaves, is pushed up through the soil. Oak and Horse Chestnut are examples.

Many tree seeds do not germinate immediately they are ripe, but require a period of dormancy. A common type of delayed germination is when the seed coat is hard and impervious, thereby precluding water uptake until it has broken down. The advantages of delayed germination are that it allows a seed to await favourable weather conditions, such as occur in late spring, or for different seeds of the same plant to germinate over a period of time.

How trees reproduce

Successive generations of tree species are established by seeds, which are the product of a process of sexual reproduction. The positive advantage of sexual reproduction is that the process allows for genes from two parents to be mixed. Half the genes in each seed will be from one parent and half from the other one. Every seed will receive a slightly different set of genes from each parent, so that it will be unique. Some seeds will be better suited to certain very slightly different conditions, so that the species will be able to exploit a wider range of sites than if the next generation were identical to their parents.

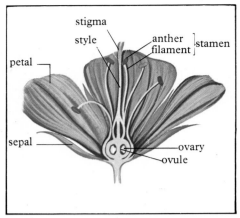

Cross-section of a typical flower.

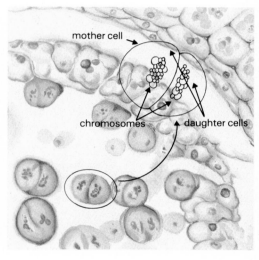

Fertilization of an egg cell by a pollen grain.

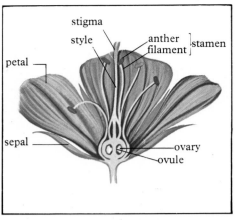

Above: cell-division (mitosis) occurring during the manufacture of pollen grains. The cell divides into two daughter cells.

Left: a honey bee transferring pollen as it collects nectar from a Pussy Willow catkin.

The exchange of genes is carried out by the flowering parts. The female or egg cells are stationary on the parent plant, but the male or pollen grains are carried from flower to flower. There are two methods of transporting the pollen grains: either the wind is used to carry them to the female flowers, or an insect (or occasionally some other animal, such as a humming bird) is the carrier.

A typical flower consists of the stalk or peduncle, a ring of sepals known as the calyx, a ring of petals called the corolla, the male parts or anthers which are on their own stalks, called filaments, and the female parts. These consist of the ovary or ovaries which are connected to the stigmas by the style.

A grain of pollen is deposited on the stigmas. There it germinates and grows down the style to the ovaries, where it fertilizes an egg. The egg then develops into a seed, with its own supply of foodstuffs to enable it to germinate and start to grow. Where there is more than one ovary, there are usually an equal number of stigmas, or lobes to the stigma.

Insect-pollinated flowers have to have at least one mechanism to attract the insect; most have two or three. Usually nectar is secreted: this is a sugar-rich solution which bees turn into honey. Scent is often used as an attractant. Often this is a pleasant fragrance; however, many flowers need to attract flies and have a smell like off-meat! Finally, the flowers are often gaudy, with brightly coloured petals that visually attract insects.

Wind-pollinated flowers, however, do not need to advertise, as it is only by chance that the wind brings pollen to them. The female flowers tend to be very small and inconspicuous, and are usually to be found at or near the top of the tree. The male flowers, which are usually catkins, are positioned lower down, so that the wind will catch the pollen and carry it up to the female flowers.

Wind-pollination requires the release of vast quantities of pollen, nearly all of which lands on anything other than a suitable flower. Insect-pollination reduces the level of waste as the pollen is transported from flower to flower. However, with a general insect-pollinator such as a bee there is no certainty that it will next alight on the right flower, and some plants have developed relationships with specific insects to reduce this waste.

Some plants have seeds with vanes or hairs attached, to catch the wind and aid in distribution to new sites. Others rely upon birds or animals collecting seeds to eat, and either dropping a few or not eating all the cache. Still others use explosive mechanisms to scatter the seeds away from the parent, but these are mainly herbs. Many trees surround the seeds with a pleasant-tasting covering. The seeds are either eaten and passed through the animal's gut unharmed, or scattered as inedible.

Right: the conspicuous yellow flowers of *Acacia confusa* awaiting the attentions of insects to effect cross-pollination. The leaf-like structures are not true leaves, but flattened petioles or 'phyllodes'.

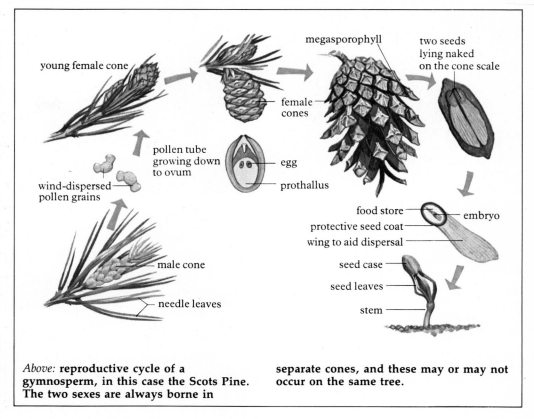

Above: **reproductive cycle of a gymnosperm, in this case the Scots Pine. The two sexes are always borne in** separate cones, and these may or may not occur on the same tree.

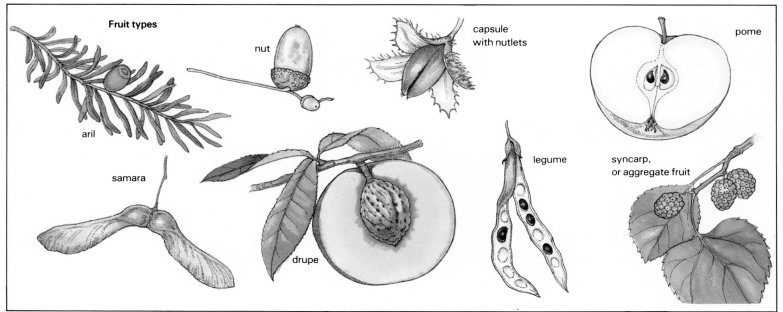

Fruit types

aril

samara

nut

drupe

capsule with nutlets

legume

pome

syncarp, or aggregate fruit

13

Roots

Roots fulfil two vital roles. These are to absorb water and minerals from the soil, and to provide anchorage. They are the great unseen part of a lofty tree, forming up to 40% of its total weight.

Roots begin with the first root or **radicle** pushed out of the seed at the start of germination. The radicle is the only geotropic root (it grows downwards into the soil). **Side-roots** soon form along the radicle, and these form the basis of the spreading root system.

Roots differ from stems and other parts of plants in a number of ways. Obviously they do not bear leaves, flowers or fruit, and they are mainly, although not exclusively, subterranean. They do not produce resting buds or nodes of growth.

A young root as it starts to grow is soft and brittle, and it is covered at the growing tip by the **root cap**, which is a collection of cells in front of the root meristem. The root cap protects the meristem, and it is continually worn away and replaced.

Behind the tip of the root are the **root hairs**. These narrow hairlike outgrowths assist in the uptake of water and nutrients from the soil. Root hairs may increase the surface area of the root by up to eighteen times. They are short-lived, persisting for only a few days or weeks. Behind the short zone of root hairs the process of secondary thickening begins. This turns the root into a tough woody structure, where the uptake of water and nutrients is reduced.

Roots can only grow under certain conditions. They will not grow through heavily compacted soils, and a badly compacted layer in the soil profile will block further growth unless there is a crack through which they can penetrate. Roots of most trees will not grow in very waterlogged sites because the air spaces in the soil are filled by water, and the roots are unable to obtain the oxygen they need. Neither are roots able to grow in or through dry soil. They are not, therefore, able positively to search for moisture, but are only able to grow through moist soil. For all these reasons root systems are rarely more than 1m deep.

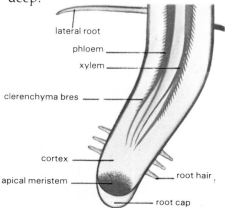

Above: **vertical section through a root, showing the growing point and the developing phloem and xylem.**

lateral root
phloem
xylem
clerenchyma bres
cortex
apical meristem
root hair
root cap

Top: **a fallen Beech tree with its root system exposed. The anchorage provided by tree roots is highly effective and sights such as this are uncommon.**

Above: **the habit of a tree as seen above ground does not reflect the arrangement of its roots beneath. Tree roots spread horizontally and do not extend more than 1 metre deep except in special circumstances.**

Roots of nearly all trees are involved in a form of symbiosis, or living-together, with fungal species. The fungus-root association is called **mycorrhiza**, and the fungal strands grow over, between or through the cells of the finer roots and extend out into the soil. The fungus absorbs nutrients and water from the soil and passes these on to the tree. In return it obtains sugars and other products of photosynthesis. Root hairs are always absent from mycorrhizal roots.

Root systems will only extend in directions that are favourable to root growth, but a given size of healthy tree will have a more than adequate root system. If the roots are prevented from going in one direction they will probably compensate by growing further in other directions.

The tree is anchored by the roots because of the vast quantities of soil with which they are in contact. As an inadequate rule of thumb, the roots will extend in a circle the radius of which is 1–1½ times the height of the tree, and usually to between 60cm and 1m down. An 18-metre Oak tree may be in contact with over 2500 tons of soil, yet itself weigh less than 10 tons.

Top: **a mature Scots Pine with its root system partially exposed.**

Right: **fruit bodies of the Fly Agaric, a mycorrhizal fungus.**

Trees and climate

A tree is rooted in one spot for life, and climate therefore has a very pronounced and long-term impact on all trees.

The **sun** is the major influencer of climate: apart from a very small amount of geothermal energy, it is the only energy source in our natural world. The energy contained in the sun's rays is mainly used as heat. With every 10°C rise in temperature the rate of a chemical reaction doubles, and photosynthesis and respiration are essentially chemical processes. Too much heat, like too little, can cause death, and sun-scorch of young seedlings is a frequent cause of seedling failure.

Plants need water to survive and grow. The amount of **rainfall** and the timing of its arrival are major factors determining the type and extent of vegetation. Trees are rarely found where the total annual precipitation is less than 20cm except along the banks of rivers, around oases or where fog provides water directly to the leaves.

The timing of the precipitation can have a major influence on tree type, particularly if the rain is in short supply. In the temperate regions of the world, total precipitation may be adequate but plants may grow more slowly than they have the potential to do, due to seasonal shortages.

The form of precipitation is also important. Very heavy rain, such as occurs in thunderstorms, causes extensive run-off and erosion. However, light rain may not do much good either: unless at least 2.5mm falls at one time it is unlikely that any will reach the forest floor and wet the soil.

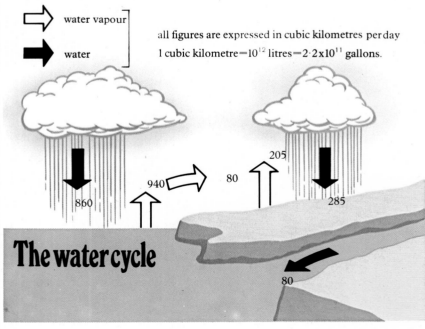

Wind has two main effects, in addition to dispersing pollen and seeds. First, in very windy sites it mechanically shapes the tree, giving it a pronounced lean to downwind. Its other effect is to bring air across the plant's surface. At very low wind speeds this is beneficial, as it replenishes the carbon dioxide used in photosynthesis. At higher wind velocities it causes drying or desiccation of soft plant tissues. The tree therefore has to work to replace the water lost, and growth is slowed.

Frost is a limiting climatic feature. It can cause damage either by occurring unexpectedly in spring or early autumn, or by its sheer intensity during winter. Frost damages the cells of soft tissues. Freezing causes ice particles to form between the cells, removing water from them. The ice may rupture the links between cells, but damage is more often caused by quick thawing, i.e. when water is made available at too fast a rate for the cells to reabsorb it. If the cell contents themselves freeze, the cell wall may be ruptured.

In advance of winter, temperate trees reduce their activity and their cell contents become more concentrated, so that freezing point is substantially lowered; but severe winter cold may still cause damage. Also, damage may result from

Above: **wind is an important environmental factor determining tree shape. Trees growing in sites with a continuous prevailing wind from one direction have longer, healthier branches on the leeward side, so that the crown appears to be blowing with the wind; this is due mainly to the fact that young buds exposed to prevailing winds are liable to be killed off.**

Diagram showing the water cycle in the world's climate: approximately 285 cubic kilometres per day fall on land surfaces as a whole. Where water is insufficient trees simply do not grow.

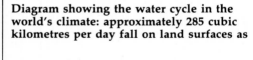

water vapour

water

all figures are expressed in cubic kilometres per day
1 cubic kilometre=10^{12} litres=$2 \cdot 2 \times 10^{11}$ gallons.

205

940

80

80

860

285

80

The water cycle

what is, in effect, freeze-drying of the plant tissues in dry cold, particularly if it is windy. Under these conditions the tree is unable to replace the water lost by the twigs.

Plant hardiness is governed by the type, extent and duration of cold. This is not purely a consequence of latitude but is influenced by other factors, such as whether the climate is based on winds coming in from the sea and is hence a maritime climate (as in Britain) or on winds coming in over land and is a continental climate (as in Siberia). Most Siberian plants do not thrive in Britain, not because it is too cold for them, but because they are tempted into early growth in spring and then damaged by regular spring frosts.

Right: **extreme winds can cause havoc even with healthy well-rooted trees.**

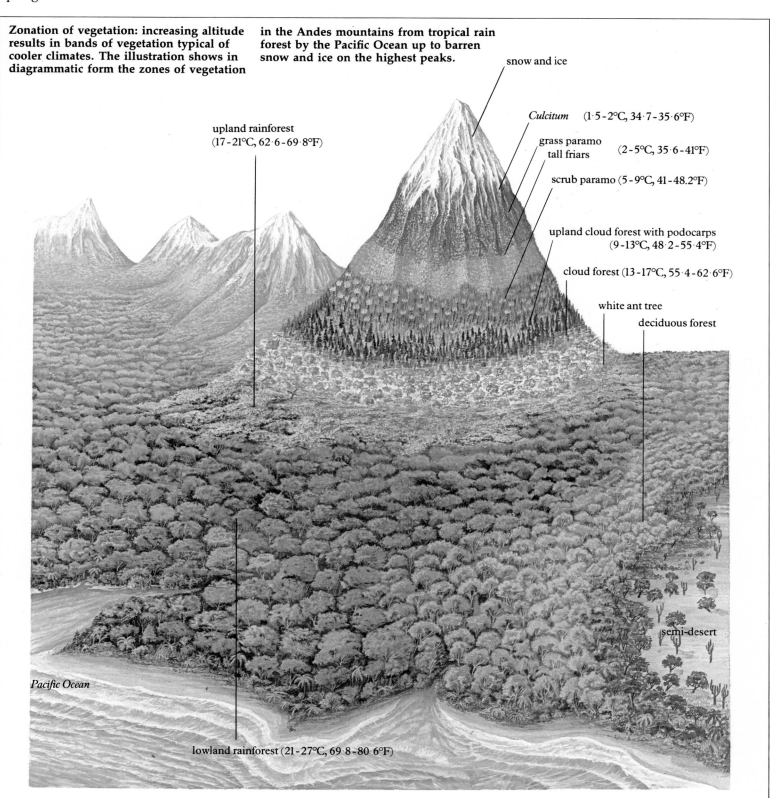

Zonation of vegetation: increasing altitude results in bands of vegetation typical of cooler climates. The illustration shows in diagrammatic form the zones of vegetation in the Andes mountains from tropical rain forest by the Pacific Ocean up to barren snow and ice on the highest peaks.

snow and ice

Culcitum (1·5-2°C, 34·7-35·6°F)

grass paramo
tall friars (2-5°C, 35·6-41°F)

scrub paramo (5-9°C, 41-48.2°F)

upland rainforest (17-21°C, 62·6-69·8°F)

upland cloud forest with podocarps (9-13°C, 48·2-55·4°F)

cloud forest (13-17°C, 55·4-62·6°F)

white ant tree

deciduous forest

semi-desert

Pacific Ocean

lowland rainforest (21-27°C, 69·8-80·6°F)

Tree nutrition

Trees use simple chemicals to build complex organic compounds by an assortment of chemical reactions, starting with photosynthesis. This section looks at these processes and at how the energy and chemicals are obtained.

Soft plant tissues are mainly water, and even apparently 'dry' fresh timber will contain over 50% water. Water is mainly absorbed from the soil by the roots, although some is taken in directly by the leaves.

Carbon, oxygen and hydrogen are the main elements in trees. The carbon and oxygen are derived from atmospheric carbon dioxide, which is present as 0.3% of the earth's atmosphere; it is absorbed directly by the leaves. The hydrogen is from water.

Sugars are made in the process of photosynthesis, which can be expressed simply by the following equation:

$$6\,CO_2 + 6\,H_2O \xrightarrow[\text{Enzymes}]{\text{Energy from sunlight}} C_6H_{12}O_6 + 6\,O_2$$

$6\,CO_2$ six molecules of carbon dioxide	$+6\,H_2O$ six molecules of water	$C_6H_{12}O_6$ sugar	$+6\,O_2$ six oxygen molecules

The sugar is used as the basic biological building block. It is combined with other sugars to form starch and cellulose, with

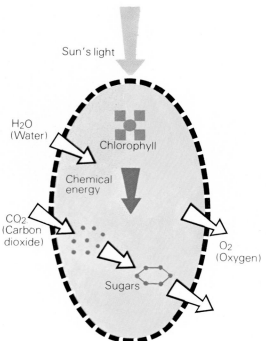

Above: **the process of photosynthesis – the chloroplasts in green plant cells contain chlorophyll, which utilizes the energy contained in light to manufacture sugars from simple materials such as water and carbon dioxide. Oxygen is a by-product.**

nitrogen to form amino acids and proteins and with other elements to form the full complement of products which are a tree.

The main elements of plant nutrition are nitrogen, phosphorus, potassium, sulphur, calcium and magnesium; but a number of other elements are equally vital, if in smaller quantities.

Nitrogen comprises 78% of the earth's atmosphere, but plants cannot assimiliate gaseous nitrogen: it must be in the form of ammonia, nitrate or nitrite. Nitrogen is absorbed mainly from the soil by the tree's roots. Some plants form symbiotic relationships with bacteria in nodules on the roots. These bacteria are able to 'fix' atmospheric nitrogen and supply the plant with nitrogen compounds, in return for sugars and other nutrients. Some is returned to the soil in leaf fall. Nitrogen is essential in protein formation, and is therefore vital in all living cells.

Potassium and **phosphorus** are mineral elements derived from soil particles. Potassium is very soluble and prone to leaching, whereas phosphorus is insoluble and may be abundant, although not in a form the tree can use. Potassium and phosphorus are needed for cell-division,

---

Below: **the principal elements in all organic matter are carbon, hydrogen, oxygen and nitrogen. This illustration shows how the energy to power the cycles of these elements is provided by the sun.**

Cycles the blue-green algae set in motion

solar energy

lime-rich strata

nitrogen fixation

evapotranspiration

CO_2

CO_2

CO_2

CO_2

H_2O

H_2O

H_2O precipitation

H_2O

N_2

N_2

respiration (energy release)

photosynthesis (energy fixation)

minerals

limestone

fossil fuel combustion

nitrogen fixation

evaporation

denitrification

dissolved carbonates (CO_3)

blue-green algae

photosynthesis

denitrification

nitrates

waste the decomposers

CO_2

waste

O_2

carbonates in shells etc.

insoluble minerals

nitrates

soluble minerals

fossil fuels

detritus

in actively growing points and in ripening fruits.

Calcium is obtained from calcium carbonate and is used by all plants in the cell walls. **Sulphur** forms part of plant proteins, and appears to encourage root development. **Magnesium** is essential as a constituent of the chlorophyll molecule.

The minor or **trace elements** are needed in very small quantities – down to 0.01 part per million for molybdenum; higher concentrations are usually toxic. They include iron (used in the manufacture of chlorophyll), boron (assists in the uptake of calcium by the roots), zinc (a constituent of certain enzymes), manganese (used in enzymes and protein synthesis), copper (enzymes) and molybdenum (important in the use of nitrate and nitrite forms of nitrogen).

Many plants will not thrive in all soils because certain nutrients are available in different forms at different levels of soil alkalinity. Rhododendrons grow on acid rather than alkaline soils, because in the latter the plant absorbs too much calcium at the expense of iron. Beech, on the other hand, can thrive in both very acid and very alkaline soils.

Above: **symptoms of nutrient deficiencies in the leaves of a Poplar species. Leaves lack 1. nothing; 2. nitrogen; 3. magnesium; 4. phosphorus; 5. magnesium and nitrogen.**

Above right: **a gall-like mass of nodules on the roots of an Alder. This formation contains millions of bacteria which help the tree to fix atmospheric nitrogen; in return they receive sugars and other nutrients from the tree.**

Right: **nitrogen deficiency in a Sitka Spruce – notice the sickly yellow coloration of the foliage.**

Temperate forests

Two types of temperate forest occur within the broad bands that lie, roughly, between 35° and 60° on either side of the equator. They vary according to temperature and the amount of rainfall received.

Temperate rain forest needs at least 130cm of rain per annum, up to a maximum of 900cm, with the rainfall being evenly distributed throughout the year. Temperatures are fairly warm in winter and relatively cool in summer. Temperate rain forest is almost entirely evergreen. The best developed region is the West Coast of North America, where the forest is coniferous, with few broadleaved trees (see pages 22–23).

Temperate deciduous woodland receives less rain – usually in the range of 50cm to 200cm and occurs in regions with higher summer and lower winter temperatures than temperate rain forest. The trees are mainly broadleaved species, such as Oak, Beech, Chestnut, Maple and Hickory. The large leaves enable them to trap a high proportion of the available light in summer. However, during the winter months the temperatures are often below freezing: the tree would

Rainfall, temperature and vegetation: from the chart you can work out what type of stable vegetation originally existed in any given area.

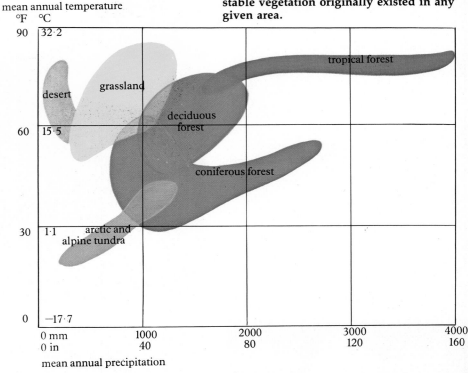

World vegetation types with their relative capital (standing crop) and their annual production of dry matter. The map is a simplified version of the one produced in 1969 by Bazilevich and Olson, two ecologists who pooled their own knowledge and some of the results of international research carried out into the relationships between climate, vegetation and productivity.

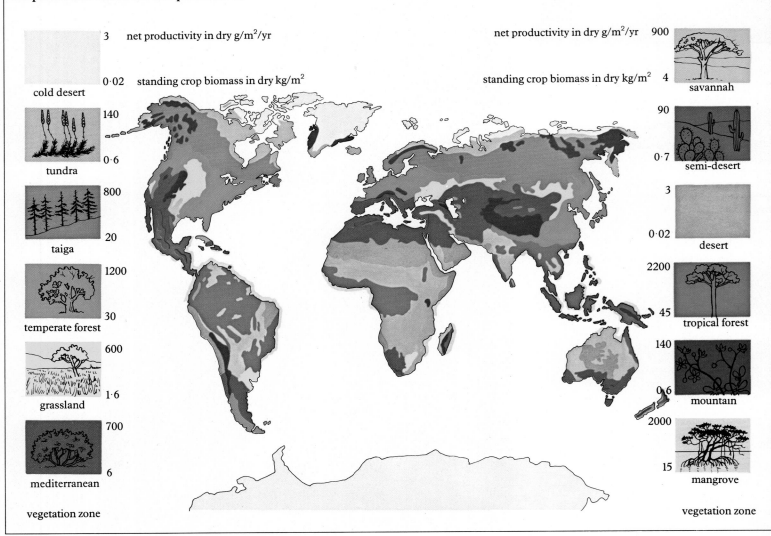

not be able to replace the water lost by these leaves and so the top parts would die from dehydration; this is why the trees shed their leaves in the autumn. Prior to losing their leaves, they withdraw a substantial part of the sugars and nutrients in them; but a significant proportion remains, and is responsible for the colours which make these woods so beautiful in the autumn. Fallen leaves are used as food by insects, woodlice, fungi, worms and so on, and the nutrients are thus returned to the soil.

This forest type is found throughout lowland Europe except the extreme north and south, in eastern North America, in temperate eastern Asia and in the southern part of Brazil. It once covered most of Europe, China and eastern North America, but only scattered remnants of virgin temperate deciduous woodland remain. It occurs naturally on rich soils (called brown earths) suitable for cultivation. Most of it has been lost to agriculture for this reason, and what has not been turned under the plough has been used for managed timber production.

Temperate deciduous forest has up to five layers. The top layer consists of the dominant trees which form a canopy 25–50m above the ground. A second layer consists of small trees, attaining perhaps 10m. The third layer is the shrub layer, with woody plants up to 3 or 5m. Near the ground is the field or herbaceous layer, consisting of grasses, spring perennials, bulbs or bracken. Along the surface, or on fallen logs, is a layer of mosses and lichens.

The trees in the canopy layer trap much of the available sunlight in mid-summer, allowing only a small amount

to reach the lower levels. Beech is more efficient than Oak in this respect and consequently Beech woodlands have poorly developed shrub and field layers. Deciduous trees keep their leaves well into the autumn months, so that little light reaches the forest floor before winter, when it is too cold for the field layers to grow. In the spring, however, the trees, particularly Oak and Ash, are slow to reclothe themselves, and many bulbs such as bluebells and other plants briefly flourish.

Temperate forest consists of up to five layers of vegetation, shown here in diagrammatic form.

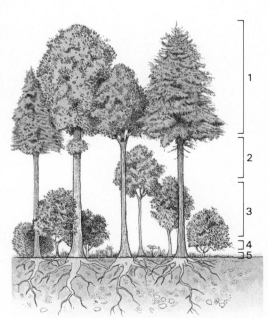

Above: **Oak woodland in the temperate belt, photographed in high summer.**

Below: **all forest types return leaf litter to the forest floor. These Beech leaves will decompose and will eventually help to provide a rich mulch for the following year's growth.**

Coniferous forests

Conifers in general outgrow broadleaved trees on soils with a low nutrient status, and/or where there are periods of drought during the growing season, and/or in regions of short growing seasons and of intense winter cold.

The leaves of most conifers are small and needle-like with a thick cuticle. Together these attributes allow conifers to conserve water – both in summer drought and winter cold. Most conifers are evergreen and the needles are usually kept for 3–5 years. This permits the trees to exploit the short growing season, as a new set of leaves need not be made in spring before photosynthesis starts. Nutrients are also recycled within the tree; there is not the annual loss of all leaves, and when leaves die there is not the compromise a deciduous tree makes between continuing photosynthesis into the autumn, and retrieving nutrients before leaves are lost in the winter.

Conifers determine in early summer of one season how many needles will be produced the following year! They are slow to respond to improvements in nutrition: if a conifer forest is fertilized no increase in growth may be apparent for up to eighteen months, whilst the effects may last for five years. Broadleaved trees, in comparison, respond more quickly.

The largest single unit of coniferous woodland is the boreal forest. This stretches for vast distances in a grand sweep around the northern hemisphere, in Canada, northern Europe and north Asia. The boreal forest is dominated by only two or three conifer species, and the only broadleaved tree present in quantity is Birch. The trees are not tall, decreasing from 30m–40m at the southern end where the boreal forest merges with the temperate deciduous forest, to little more than scattered shrubs as the forest gives way to arctic tundra.

Large shrubs are rare in the boreal forest. Instead there is a carpeting layer of dwarf shrubs up to 1m high, such as bilberries, under which is a layer of scattered herbaceous plants and mosses and lichens. In some parts Reindeer Moss (which is a lichen) is the only plant other than the forest trees.

The boreal forest experiences very cold winters and short cool summers. Rainfall is low – from 25cm – but because of the low evaporation rate it is sufficient for tree growth.

In mountain chains south of the boreal forest, conifers dominate the final zones of forest before the tree line. The forest there is similar to the boreal forest. The temperature drops by 1°C for every 170m rise in altitude, causing a shortening of the growing season as height increases. Searing dry winter winds may also induce a water shortage.

Conifers may dominate on poor sandy soils such as those found in the southeast USA. Here the rainfall is 100cm to 125cm, but as the soil is not retentive, and because of the high evaporation, conifers with their ability to withstand drought are the principal trees.

Similar conditions lead to conifers being frequent or dominant in Mediterranean climates, in southwestern USA and in other parts of the world.

Temperate rain forest is frequently dominated by coniferous trees. The forest type is found along the Pacific coast of North America, the west coast of New Zealand, Southern Chile and in southeast Australia. In the Pacific coast of North America the Coastal Redwood frequently exceeds 100m in height.

Above: **Bilberry** (*Vaccinium myrtillus*) **in its early summer form. This is often a constituent of the forest floor layer in natural woods of Scots Pine.**

Below: **natural pine woods in Scotland. These woodlands consist of open forest of large trees with a low carpet layer of small** shrubs. The Scots Pines themselves are present in many shapes and sizes.

Above: **Alpine wood of Larch extending to the tree line in Austria.**

Left: **ripening cone of Faber Fir growing in West China.**

Tropical rain forest

Tropical rain forest is an important part of the world's forest resource. However, due to incessant and destructive felling this priceless forest type may cease to exist by the year 2000.

Tropical rain forest is found in the lowland regions of the tropics wherever there is a regular and high rainfall, at the very least 150cm. The mean monthly temperature is above 25°C with little variation through the year, and the relative humidity is high. The climate of tropical rain forest is akin to a Turkish bath – warm, dark, damp and sweaty.

Tropical rain forests are a complex but very fragile ecological system. They are very productive because of the wealth of plants, but if the forest is cleared the high rainfall and poor nature of the soil soon lead to a barren site.

Unlike the boreal forest, where one or two conifer species dominate vast regions, in the tropical rain forest very many tree species are present, with perhaps only one or two specimens of each species per hectare.

Evergreen tropical rain forest is found in three parts of the world. In Asia it is found in India through Malaya to New Guinea and northern Australia, and in Africa from the Congo basin in Zaire westwards in a belt extending to Liberia. In America evergreen rain forest occurs in the Amazon basin, north to Central America and parts of the West Indies. In these regions dry periods are of limited duration.

Five layers of vegetation are discernible in evergreen rain forest. At the highest level is an irregular number of 'emergent' trees, rising far above the general canopy, and up to 60m tall. The main canopy of the forest is a more or less continuous layer of trees about 30m high. Beneath this is a third layer of small trees 10 to 15m tall. This layer is scattered and irregular, as is the shrub layer, which may include tree ferns. The field layer consists of herbs and ferns.

In addition to the five layers described there are two groups of plants attempting

Below: **the canopy of evergreen tropical rain forest remains at a uniform level, even on undulating ground, because valley trees grow taller. The uniformity of** the canopy is, however, broken by an irregular number of 'emergent' trees (not shown).

Above: **tropical rain forest in Malaya. There are so many tree species present in this forest type that any given species may be represented by only one or two specimens per hectare.**

to get a share of the light: the epiphytes and the lianas.

Epiphytic plants grow in the branches and on the stems of trees. They do not root in any soil, obtaining all their needs from the rain and what nutrients they can trap. Orchids are an important group of epiphytes, as are some ferns. In the American evergreen rain forests, Bromeliads (relatives of the pineapple) are common epiphytes.

Lianas are woody climbers which are rooted in the soil and slowly grow into the upper canopy layers, where they may extend laterally for tens of metres. Climbing plants are a particular feature of tropical rain forests.

The trees in the forest all tend to have a long round bole with thin smooth bark. At the butt the trunk is supported by narrow plank-like buttresses. The leaves are elliptic, entire and with a drip-tip to assist water run-off.

Semi-evergreen tropical rain forest occurs in parts of Africa and Asia where conditions similar to those of evergreen rain forest prevail, apart from a pronounced dry period of 4–6 months (this type of forest is common where monsoons bring the rain). During the dry period most or all of the trees lose their leaves.

Below: **epiphylls on the leaf of a Fan Palm. Palm leaves are often very large and the tough ones last for a long time, making** them an ideal perch for mini-epiphytes. This old leaf is also covered with lichens and some small mosses and liverworts.

Above: **many of the trees in tropical rain forest have huge buttressed trunks, and they are often festooned with creepers.**

Savannas

Savannas occupy large parts of the world between 5° and 20° latitude north and south of the equator. They are found in Africa on both sides of the equator, and these belts are joined by the East African highlands. In South America they are found in parts of Venezuela and in Brazil south of the Amazon. Much of Australia is covered by savanna, as are some parts of India.

Savannas are technically tropical grasslands and do not always have trees. However, most do, and the trees may be considered an essential element of the vegetation type. The density of the tree cover depends upon the amount of rainfall: if this is less than 60cm, shrubs, not trees, will form the woody top layer of the vegetation. If the rainfall exceeds 125–150cm, semi-deciduous tropical rain forest may result. Tree savanna is found between these rainfall limits.

Savannas have effectively three seasons, although each one is warm. The period when the sun is low is a relatively 'cool' period and is dry. The rains come usually in one period during the summer when the climate is moist and warm. In early summer, prior to the rains, there is a hot dry period. Savanna has considerable dry periods, which may last for up to eight months of the year.

Because savannas are in the tropics, the potential for transpiration is very high and far exceeds the available water supply. The trees therefore have to be capable of reducing their water requirements for large parts of the year if they are to survive.

Many of the trees are deciduous and lose all their leaves during the dry periods. They may replace their leaves at the end of the dry season so that the new leaves are ready to work as soon as the rains come. The new foliage of deciduous trees is often brightly coloured for several weeks before it is fully expanded and turns green.

Some of the trees are evergreen, and these have small leaves with thick cuticles to cut down on water loss.

The Baobab Tree has a novel, if odd, solution to the problem. The huge trunk and main branches are composed, in the centre, of soft spongy tissue which is able to store considerable quantities of water accumulated during the rainy season; and it is only for a few weeks at this time of year that the tree has any leaves.

Most trees in savanna forest are members of the Legume family. Species of *Acacia* are particularly frequent. The trees are not tall, rarely exceeding 20m, and the crown is Y-shaped or vase-shaped on a short trunk.

Below left: **Ghost Gums** (*Eucalyptus papuana*) **near Alice Springs, Central Australia. Ghost Gum is found over vast tracts of savanna across northern Australia and Papua New Guinea.**

Trees are only occasionally close enough to reach each other to count as woodland. Usually there is clear space around each tree, although this diminishes with increasing rainfall.

As transpiration potentially exceeds water supply, the trees may bring water up from well below the soil surface. In these conditions the soil may become very alkaline due to salts from below being deposited on the surface by evaporation.

Savanna is characterized by grass. During the dry seasons the grass withers and is very easily set alight. Fire from natural causes, such as lightning, is an ever-present threat, and this is increased when man is present. The mature trees in most savanna formations are resitant to fire damage. Most achieve this by the thickness of their bark, which insulates the living parts of the tree for long enough to survive the fire. *Eucalyptus* in Australia have the ability to regrow quickly from the stump.

Below: **vase-shaped specimens of** *Acacia* **dominate large areas of African and Australian savannas. These Fever Trees are growing in the Kenyan bush.**

Above: Acacia robusta **in flower, in an area of low rainfall where the trees are scarcely bigger than large shrubs.**

Plantation forestry

Man has been involved in forest management for very many centuries, starting with neolithic man lopping branches to feed his cattle or goats in dry periods in summer. In the course of time he has removed much of the world's natural forest cover. The development of forestry management techniques led to the current reliance upon plantations to supply a substantial part of our timber needs.

When man first harvests timber from a virgin stand he is able to cut more than the annual growth rate of the trees can meet, because no one has previously cut any. However, if after he has felled all the trees in the forest he wishes to manage the area to maximize the amount of timber he can extract, he is only able to cut over a period of years the volume of timber which has grown over that period. In the short term, therefore, felling a virgin forest produces a higher volume of timber than a managed forest, as both the annual increase and the accumulated timber are taken at once.

The problem then facing forest managers is restocking the land with trees.

Natural regeneration is a possible way, if suitable parent trees are available in the area. In many circumstances natural regeneration may work very well – after all, it was how the original forest arose. However, very often the conditions that follow the felling of an existing crop are not the same as those under which the

Right: **a dense monoculture of Scots Pine for timber production – compare with the natural pine wood shown on page 22.**

crop arose. In some cases in nature *A* follows *B* follows *A*, and therefore natural regeneration may not produce the desired effect – at least not for two or three centuries!

Man's demand for timber is ever increasing. We therefore need to manage forests to produce as much timber of the required quality as is feasible in the circumstances. In many cases the natural crop does not fit the requirements, and therefore there is no option but to plant rather than let nature take its course.

In establishing a plantation the basic objective is to plant a number of trees into conditions in which they can thrive, and then tend them so that they do. For economic and practical reasons the trees used in forestry are around 30cm in height when planted – larger trees are often slow to start growing, as well as being costly and bulky. The newly-planted tree will probably need weeding. Unless the site is a good one the ground may have been ploughed, but only in rows, as complete ploughing is usually not economically justified. Together these factors dictate that the trees are planted in straight lines.

Normally, unless the crop is an especially valuable one, many more trees are planted than will survive until the final felling. There are several reasons for this. Some trees will fail, others will be damaged by birds or animals or accidents so that they are not suitable final crop trees. Others will be removed in thinning operations. Also, when the young trees join their crowns together they shade out the ground vegetation: they no longer require weeding and they experience a boost in growth following the removal of the competition. It is desirable to promote this as early as possible.

After a period lasting a number of years, called the rotation, the trees are felled and replaced.

Opposite page, top: **young rubber trees in a Malaysian plantation.**

Opposite page, bottom: **a nursery full of young Coconut Palms.**

Right: **coppice with standards is an old form of forest management. The standards are cut to provide timber and the coppice cut every five to twenty years for poles, pinewood or bark. In this case the poles stacked against the tree have been cut for use as thatching spars.**

29

Trees in commerce

Wood may appear at first glance to be the obvious economic use of trees, but it is only one of a dozen or so ways in which they have a significant commercial impact upon man.

Wood may in any case be used in a variety of ways. About half the quantity used in the world is burnt as firewood. For much of the Third World it provides the fuel with which food is cooked, and in some parts the wood used for cooking the meal is more costly than the meal itself.

Timber is a versatile material and has a very satisfactory feel and appearance. However, it is relatively uneconomical in terms of wood usage: when a tree trunk is sawn into planks, these consist of only about half the original volume of the log. The rest is accounted for by offcuts to make the round log square, by the proportion turned into sawdust and wood shavings, and by that lost due to natural defects.

However, wood can be processed to give boards with many of the advantages of timber but fewer drawbacks. Plywood, chipboard, and fibre board are examples of such boards.

Veneers are produced like plywood, but with only one layer of the decorative veneer stuck on to plywood or chipboard. This gives the quality appearance at a bargain price.

Woodwool is thin streamers of wood made by shaving a log. It is used in insulation and for packaging.

But most of the wood each one of us uses is as paper. Paper is made from cellulose fibres which are an important component of wood. Cotton is almost pure cellulose, and old cotton rags make the best papers. Wood, however, is not pure cellulose. The quality of paper depends upon the effort put into making the wood pulp into purer cellulose.

Above: **rubber tapping in Malaysia. Latex – the raw material which gives rubber – is the sap of rubber trees.**

Right: **pine trees are tapped for their resin, which is quaintly called 'naval stores'. Present-day uses include turpentine and resin (used as a 'sizing' or filling agent in quality papers).**

Two main methods of paper-making from wood exist. In the chemical process the non-cellulose elements of wood are removed chemically. This produces good paper, although the price is high. The quality of the paper is improved by adding various agents, such as China clay, to make it glossier, thicker or take ink better. Cheap papers such as newsprint are made by the grinding of trees into the strands of cellulose. As the non-cellulose elements are not removed the paper is of low quality.

Trees produce food, mostly from fruits such as apples, oranges or nuts. However there are several other ways in which trees provide food. The leaves of many trees are edible, if only a few are agreeable to the palate. They have been used to provide feed for cattle and goats

since neolithic times. They also indirectly provide honey – usually from the flowers, but also from the honeydew excreted by many sap-sucking aphids.

Bark provides a number of products. It is being increasingly used in horticulture as a longer-lasting substitute for peat, but the two traditional benefits are tannin for the tanning industry and bast for rope-making.

Trees provide resins and latex, which are tapped from the tree by the cutting of the bark. Resins yield turpentine and similar products, whilst latex is the raw material for rubber.

Trees can be planted so as to form a windbreak, which can be especially useful where the seasonal cycle includes a long dry spell, when winds can blow around vast quantities of dust. They will also bind soil to prevent erosion, and this is very important around dams, as uncontrolled erosion of the catchment area can soon cause the lake to silt up.

Trees may be planted or left in position to provide shade and shelter, such as here over a tea plantation in southern India.

Plants and animals associated with trees

Left: **the Crested Tit searches for insects at all levels in Scots Pines. Its favourite breeding niche is the decaying stumps of dead pines where there are both holes and crevices to nest in and the larvae of wood-boring insects with which to feed the young.**

the benefit is mutual, if not equal, and those where the animals are making a grab.

The best example of a mutually beneficial relationship is provided by insects such as the honey bee, which obtains either protein (as pollen) or sugar-rich nectar from the flowers. In the process the bee transfers pollen from flower to flower, thereby accomplishing cross-pollination.

Trees use animals in a variety of ways to distribute their seeds. The relationship usually revolves around the tree providing a food source such as nuts in antici-

Trees are an essential part of the ecosystem wherever they are present, providing homes and shelter for many different plants and animals.

Epiphytes (plants which live in the crowns of trees) are quite common in damp tropical climates and infrequent in dry cold ones. They obtain all their needs from the air, from rainwater and from what collects in crevices in the tree. Many epiphytes in tropical regions are Orchids; others, the Bromeliads (related to pineapple) collect water in the angles at the base of the leaves. Ferns are epiphytes in all regions where the climate is sufficiently moist. In drier areas mosses and lichens are frequent.

There are also a number of parasitic plants, of which the best known example is probably Mistletoe (*Viscum album*). The European Mistletoe is only partially parasitic: it obtains its water and nutrients from the host tree, but makes sugars by photosynthesis like other plants. Some American species obtain all their needs from the host. Trees also provide a habitat for mycorrhizal fungi (see page 15).

Animals obtain two main services from trees – food and shelter. The relationships can be divided into those in which

Above: **English Oak is the recorded home of nearly three hundred species of insect, including the one which caused these leaf galls.**

Left: **the bark of this low coppiced oak is covered in a layer of lichens which testify to the humidity and the relatively unpolluted air.**

Opposite page, bottom: **Bromeliads and other epiphytes 'hitch-hiking' a space near the sun, up in the canopy of tropical rain forest.**

pation that a few seeds will be distributed. The common fruits such as apple have an edible flesh around the seeds, while large seeds such as acorns rely on birds or animals carrying seeds away to store and subsequently not finding them. Some seeds, such as May or Yew are eaten by a bird or animal: they pass through the gut and are then planted, ready to grow, in an individual supply of manure.

Many animals provide little or no ben-efit to the tree, using it purely as a food source, grazing the foliage and twigs as cows graze a meadow. Mostly these are insects but other animals range from voles – which graze the bark in severe winters, to giraffes, which eat the reach-able foliage.

Finally trees provide shelter for many animals. The shelter may be protection from predators, such as when birds nest in the branches, or protection from the desiccating effects of cold wind.

Top and above left: **fruit bodies of fungi on the outside of tree trunks – the fungal mycelium is digesting the wood from within. The top picture shows Beefsteak Fungus, the lower one Razor-strop Fungus or Birch Polypore.**

Above: **Red Squirrels are abundant over Europe and Asia, but in some areas of deciduous woodland they have been replaced by the Grey Squirrel. The Red Squirrel prefers coniferous woodland.**

Evolution, or the relationships of plants

Tertiary and Quaternary

65

Cretaceous

136

Jurassic

190

Triassic

225

Permian

280

Carboniferous

345

Devonian

395

millions of years ago

flowering plants

cycads

ginkgos

conifers

ferns

Bennettitales

horsetails

lycopods

seed ferns

Cordaitales

the primitives

The Earth is believed to have been formed 4–5000 million years ago but the evolution of plants has occurred within the last 600 million years. For the first 150 million years of this period all the plants were simple ones, such as algae and fungi, but about four hundred million years back the first land plants began to appear. They were liverworts and mosses but these do not concern us, as they were, and their successors still are, non-woody.

The 'simplest' group of woody plants are the ferns and horsetails. In fact few woody ferns and no woody horsetails survive, but in the past, particularly in the carboniferous period when our coal and oil reserves were formed, they were an important group of plants.

Ferns do not reproduce directly but by way of a second or alternate generation. It is this alternate or 'gametophyte' generation, which is un-fernlike in appearance, that produces the next fern or 'sporophyte' generation. The evolutionary sequence of land plants is a reduction in size, if not in importance, of the gametophyte generation.

After the ferns, the next step is *Ginkgo biloba* – the Maidenhair Tree and its extinct relatives. *Ginkgo* has been around for some 200 million years and fossil leaves virtually indistinguishable from the living species are often found. The main advance of *Ginkgo* over the ferns is that the sporophyte generation is started by a seed with food reserves rather than by a minute spore. The species is therefore able to grow on less hospitable sites than the ferns. *Ginkgo* has motile spermatozoa which effect fertilization of the egg by swimming through their own nuptial pool; this is considered a primitive feature.

Left: **a diagrammatic portrayal of the often accepted relationships between evolution, time and extinction. The thickness of the band at any time indicates the relative diversity of the group as present in the fossil record.**

The conifers have dispensed with free-swimming spermatozoa and are thus placed at a more advanced level than *Ginkgo*. Fertilization is effected by the pollen grains landing amongst the cone scales, and growing through the tissues in a pollen tube which neatly deposits the sperm beside the egg cell.

The conifers belong to the group of plants known as 'gymnosperms'. Literally this translates as 'naked seeds'. The developing seed is always external to the parent plant, although enclosed within the expanded cone scales.

The most advanced group of plants have devised a system for protecting the embryo within the tissues of the mother plant. These are the flowering plants or 'angiosperms', meaning 'hidden seeds', as the protection hides the embryo. The angiosperms have, in fact, reduced the gametophyte generation to a mere eight cells within the plant's life history.

The angiosperms have continued to evolve (as have the other groups in a number of ways) and the monocotyledons – with only one seed-leaf, may be more advanced than the dicotyledons, which have two seed-leaves. The monocots include the palms, bulbs and grasses whilst the dicots contain trees, shrubs, flowering plants and annuals.

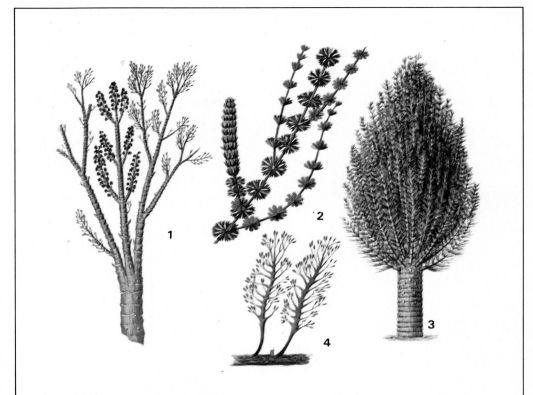

Woody horsetails became extinct millions of years ago, and only a few non-woody species survive. These pictures are an artist's impression of how they may have appeared. 1. shoot of *Calamophyton:* **2.** *Sphenophyllostachys;* **3.** *Crucicalamites;* **4.** *Protohyenia janovii.*

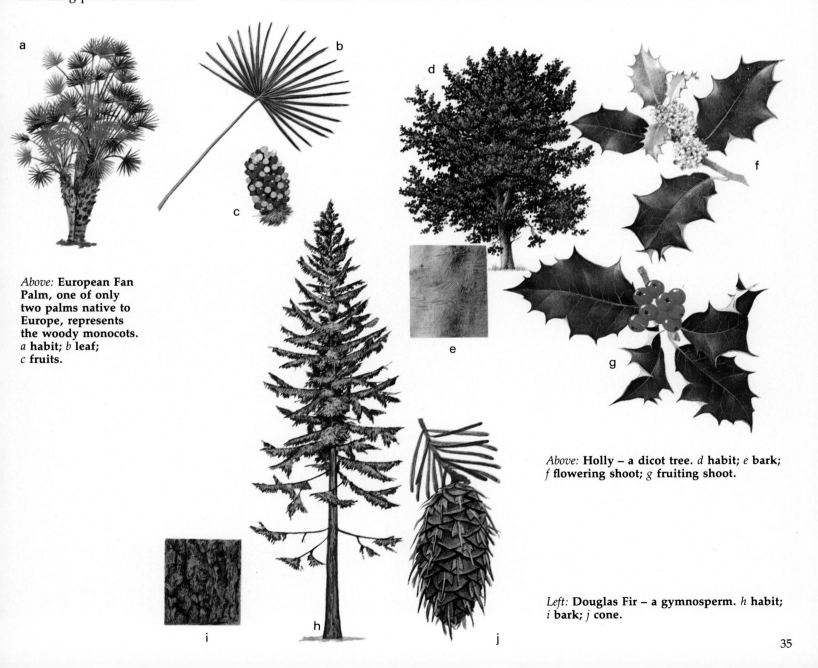

Above: **European Fan Palm, one of only two palms native to Europe, represents the woody monocots.** *a* **habit;** *b* **leaf;** *c* **fruits.**

Above: **Holly – a dicot tree.** *d* **habit;** *e* **bark;** *f* **flowering shoot;** *g* **fruiting shoot.**

Left: **Douglas Fir – a gymnosperm.** *h* **habit;** *i* **bark;** *j* **cone.**

Distribution of the world's trees

The tree species included in this book are representative of several distinct distribution patterns. At the global level there are families such as the Beeches (Fagaceae), the Elms (Ulmaceae) and the Cypresses (Cupressaceae) which span the continents on both sides of the equator. The Fagaceae, for example, which is represented in the northern hemisphere by Quercus, Castanea and Fagus, is an extremely ancient family probably dating back to the early Cretaceous period. The closest relative of the Beech genus Fagus, so widespread in the northern hemisphere, is the Southern Beech genus Nothofagus, equally widespread in the temperate areas of Australia, New Zealand, South America and the mountains of New Guinea and New Caledonia. The divergence of these two genera probably dates back to the break up of the ancient supercontinent (Pangaea).

By contrast, some genera are strictly confined to either the New or the Old World. A classical Old World pattern for a relict distribution is seen in the Wingnut genus Pterocarya, which has one species in the Caucasus, one in Japan and six in China. Another interesting example is the diverse genus Cotoneaster, which has some seventy species entirely restricted to the Old World mountain ranges. Much less diverse but showing another Old World distribution pattern is the genus Laburnum, which has three reasonably widespread species in southern Europe and western Asia.

Within the northern hemisphere there are only a few species of tree, such as the Common Juniper Juniperus communis, known to be widespread throughout Europe, Asia and North America. Nevertheless, there are quite a number of widely different genera which are represented by closely related species in the two separate land masses. For example, the Eastern and Western Plane Trees, respectively Platanus orientalis and P. occidentalis, are now widely separated in eastern North America and the eastern Mediterranean region, but probably formed continuous populations at a time before the continents drifted apart. Despite a long separation, a hybrid between the two species, the commonly cultivated London Plane P. x acerifolia is a living testament to the biological similarity of the parent species.

Ginkgo and the Yew family

Ginkgo or Maidenhair Tree (*Ginkgo biloba*) has a long pedigree extending back over 200 million years, according to paleantologists. It is a gymnosperm, but differs in a number of important characters from the conifers. It is in its own family (Ginkgoaceae) and even its own order (Ginkgoales). The principal difference from the conifers is that pollination of the ovule is achieved by motile or free-swimming sperm cells. Fertilization is not achieved until the autumn, by which time the seed may have fallen to the ground.

The leaves open yellow-green in the spring, becoming rich bright green and finally turning clear yellow or gold in autumn. Two types of shoot are produced. Short and very slow-growing shoots are made along old twigs. Extension growth is made by long shoots, which have alternate leaves. The bark is dull grey and composed of a coarse network of crossing ridges and fissures. In old trees bosses develop and slowly grow down the trunk. The crown is usually very upright with a strong leading shoot. Short branches form all around the trunk, and every now and then one grows faster and longer, giving in trees up to a hundred years old a rather interesting and gaunt crown.

The fruits and flowers are carried on the short shoots of separate male and female trees. Female trees produce globular or ovoid 3cm fruits. The kernel is delightful roasted, but the outer fleshy part emits a putrid stench which lingers on the fingers.

Planted in 1762, 200 years on this Ginkgo at Kew Gardens is in excellent health. This tree is a male and therefore does not produce fruit.

Below: **fossilized Ginkgo leaves, showing that this unique species has survived virtually unaltered for around 150 million years.**

Ginkgo or Maidenhair Tree (*Ginkgo biloba*): *a* **habit;** *b* **bark;** *c* **catkins;** *d* **leaves;** *e* **fruit.**

Above: **leaves and fruit of the Californian Nutmeg** (*Torreya californica*), **an American member of the Yew family.**

Nearly every part of the yew tree is poisonous, the one exception being the brightly coloured aril. This is sweet, almost sickly so, and is readily devoured by birds and animals. The seed itself is very poisonous, but the seed coat is thick and hard, and unless crushed by the teeth the seed will pass through the gut. This passage assists both in germination of the seed and in dispersal of the species, as migrant birds may cover vast distances whilst carrying seeds.

Common Yew (*Taxus baccata*) is very tolerant of shade and competition. It is one of the very few plants which can grow and thrive beneath Beech, and like Beech it flourishes on both acid and alkaline sites. It is very long lived and relatively slow growing. Ages of up to 1000 years are often quoted, with girth to 10m. However, the old trees are invariably hollow, and accurate counts of tree rings are not possible.

Irish Yew is a fastigiate form of Yew in which all the shoots have radial leading shoot foliage.

Until the last Ice Age, Ginkgo was found in Europe, but in the wild it has only survived in remote parts of southeast China. It was adopted as a sacred tree by Buddhist monks in the first millenia A.D. and planted around their temples. It may owe its survival to this practice; it is not certain whether it still survives in a wild state. It is an extremely long-lived tree, without any foliage, wood or bark pests.

The **Yews** (*Taxus*) are a group of about ten species. As a group they are very widely distributed, being found throughout Europe, in North Africa, across North America and throughout temperate Asia as far south as the Celebes Islands of Indonesia. The group is characterized by the fleshy aril of the fruit. Yew trees are either male or female, and fruit is only found on female trees. The aril starts as a thin hard layer of green which covers the lower part of the seed, developing into a juicy and fleshy, bright red, cup-like structure. At 1cm the aril is about a third longer than the seed, which it conceals in a deep cavity.

Common Yew (*Taxus baccata*): *a* **habit;** *b* **male flowers;** *c* **fruits. Cow-tail Pine** (*Cephalotaxus harringtonia*): *d* **habit;** *e* **fruits. This species is similar to the Common Yew although the Cow-tail Pines are regarded as a separate family (Cephalotaxaceae).**

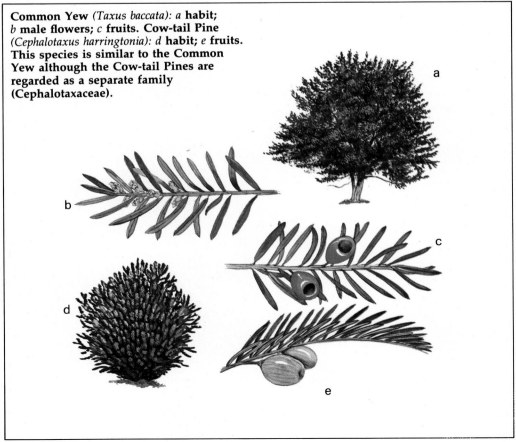

The Redwood family

The Redwood family (Taxodiaceae) contains the tallest and largest trees in the world. The family consists of ten separate genera but only seventeen species; no genus has more than three species.

The Redwood (*Sequoia sempervirens*) is at 112m (368ft) the tallest tree in the world. Claims that other trees, such as Eucalypts and Douglas Firs, have exceeded 120m have never been substantiated.

The Redwood, or Coastal Redwood, only grows well where the rainfall is between 100cm and 250cm, although it will tolerate less. It is restricted in nature to a narrow band along the Pacific coast of central and northern California and just extends into southern Oregon. There the climate is mild in winter, when most of the rain falls, and not particularly hot in summer. However, fog is frequent during the summer months and provides a significant proportion of the tree's water requirements. The technical problems the tree has to overcome in moving water and nutrients from the roots at ground level to a height of over 100m must be formidable.

The tallest trees are only found in flat valley bottoms but these account for only 2% of the Redwood forest. The remaining trees are merely tall.

The Wellingtonia, Big Tree or Sierra Redwood (*Sequoiadendron giganteum*) is the largest living thing in the world. The biggest of all, General Sherman, is estimated to weigh 6000 tonnes, is 83m tall with a basal diameter of 10m, yet grew from a seed weighing one two-hundredth of a gram. Wellingtonia is confined to six dozen scattered groves in the Sierra Nevada, California, at 1500 to 2500m. The rainfall is lower than in the Coastal Redwood zone and the climate is more severe, with hot summers and cold winters.

Both trees are evergreen. However, the family contains three of the five deciduous conifer genera, including the Dawn Redwood (*Metasequoia glyptostroboides*) and the Swamp or Bald Cypress (*Taxodium distichum*).

Right: **General Sherman, a Wellingtonia – Daddy of them all, the largest living thing on earth. 83 metres tall, 10 metres butt diameter and weighing a mere 6000 tonnes!**

Opposite page, bottom: **Dawn Redwood** (*Metasequioa glyptostroboides*) **is a Chinese fossil tree only discovered in 1944. It is deciduous and has an attractive fibrous bark.**

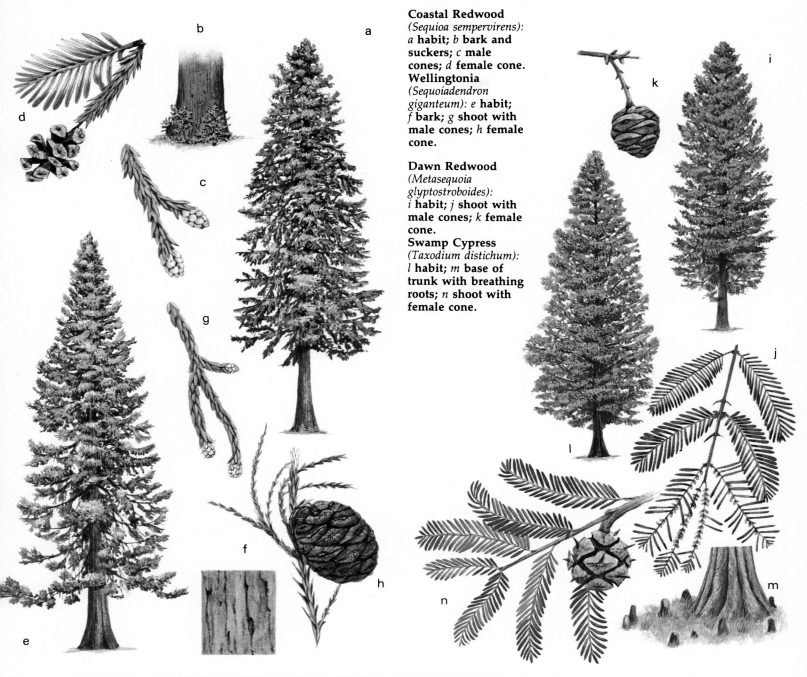

Coastal Redwood
(Sequioa sempervirens):
a **habit;** *b* **bark and**
suckers; *c* **male**
cones; *d* **female cone.**
Wellingtonia
(Sequoiadendron
giganteum): *e* **habit;**
f **bark;** *g* **shoot with**
male cones; *h* **female**
cone.

Dawn Redwood
(Metasequoia
glyptostroboides):
i **habit;** *j* **shoot with**
male cones; *k* **female**
cone.
Swamp Cypress
(Taxodium distichum):
l **habit;** *m* **base of**
trunk with breathing
roots; *n* **shoot with**
female cone.

The Swamp Cypress is confined to southeast USA. It forms a tree up to 30m high and is capable of growing in swamps, with water swilling around the trunk. In these conditions it develops special roots called 'pneumatophores' or 'knees' which grow above the water level and assist in supplying the roots with oxygen. The Swamp Cypress is capable of growing in almost any soil, including dry ones, but 'knees' are not produced in normal soils.

The Dawn Redwood was only discovered in 1944 in a remote part of central China, and is now planted more often than other Redwoods. Like the Swamp Cypress it will grow in any soil and prefers damp sites, but cannot grow in swamps.

Swamp Cypress and Dawn Redwood both have their leaves set on the shoots in fernlike sprays. Most of these shoots are lost with the leaves in the autumn, but on the permanent shoots the individual leaves are lost.

The Cypress, Monkey Puzzle and Podocarp families

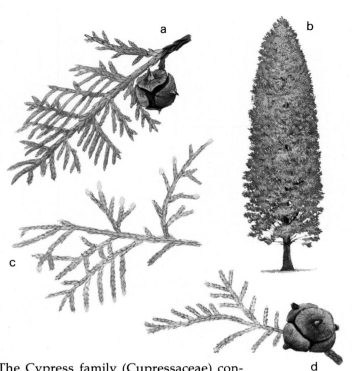

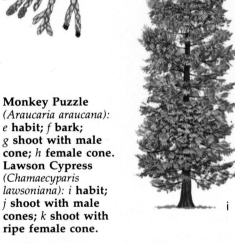

The Cypress family (Cupressaceae) consists of a number of different genera, most of which have only a few species. The foliage is distinctive: except in *Juniperus* it is always in opposite pairs and usually scale-like, although in juvenile plants the leaves are awl-like.

The family is divided into three on the basis of the cones. Most genera have rounded cones with shield-like scales, and look like miniature sputniks. The Cypresses (*Cupressus*, *Chamaecyparis* and *Cupressocyparis*) belong to this group. *Thuja* species have upright oval cones with scales hinged at the base. Juniper cones are a modified version of the for-

mer types; the scales are not woody but become fleshy or mealy.

Lawson Cypress (*Chamaecyparis lawsoniana*) is the commonest Cypress. In the wild it is found only in a restricted part of northwest America. It has produced very many variants or cultivars but can nearly always be identified by the pendent tip, the small cones and flat sprays of foliage.

Italian Cypress (*Cupressus sempervirens*) has cones measuring over 2cm which take two years to ripen. Its habit is narrow and upright. Smooth Cypress and

Nootka Cypress (*Chamaecyparis nootkatensis*): *a* **shoot with female cone.** **Leyland Cypress** (*Cupressocyparis leylandii*): *b* **habit;** *c* **shoot with male cones;** *d* **female cone.**

Monkey Puzzle (*Araucaria araucana*): *e* **habit;** *f* **bark;** *g* **shoot with male cone;** *h* **female cone.** **Lawson Cypress** (*Chamaecyparis lawsoniana*): *i* **habit;** *j* **shoot with male cones;** *k* **shoot with ripe female cone.**

Monterey Cypress (*C. glabra* and *C. macrocarpa*) are other species in cultivation. Leyland Cypress (x *Cupressocyparis leylandii*) is a fast-growing hybrid of Monterey Cypress and Nootka Cypress (*Chamaecyparis nootkatensis*).

Western Red Cedar (*Thuja plicata*) is distinguished by its fresh yellow-green foliage, which is delightfully scented. Incense Cedar (*Calocedrus decurrens*) is closely related but has two pairs of scale leaves brought together almost into a whorl of four.

Juniper (*Juniperus communis*) is one of a number which have only awl-like foliage; in Juniper it is in whorls of three. Other Junipers, such as Chinese Juniper and Pencil Cedar (*J. chinensis* and *J. virginiana*) have both scale leaves and awl leaves in pairs or threes.

The **Monkey Puzzle** family (Araucariaceae) consists of only two genera and is restricted to the southern hemisphere.

The Kauri Pine (*Agathis australis*) is a

Common Juniper (*Juniperus communis*): *l* **habit;** *m* **male flowers;** *n* **female flowers;** *o* **upper side of leaf;** *p* **fruit.**

dominant constituent of the forests of North Island, New Zealand. The enormous trees with long straight cylindrical boles were soon pillaged by the settlers for their quality timber.

The Monkey Puzzle (*Araucaria araucana*) is native to southern Chile. It has prickly broad leaves – totally unlike normal conifer needles – set in spirals on the shoot. Trees are very whorled in appearance and either male or female. The cones ripen over two or three years to release large seeds which taste like chestnuts.

The **Podocarp** family (Podocarpaceae) is mainly southern hemisphere in distribution. It is a varied group of plants which are ecologically important in their native regions, but as these are mainly tropical only a few are seen in cultivation.

Podocarpus is the main genus. Willow Podocarp (*P. salignus*) is a Chilean species with long narrow leaves. It has an orange or red-brown shaggy bark. *Phyllocladus* is an Australasian genus. Instead of leaves its photosynthetic area is in cladodes, which are leaf-like shoots. The true leaves are scale-like and brown.

Above: **Yellow-woods** (*Widdsingtonia*), **a small South African group of Cypresses, tower above the surrounding forest.**

Below: **the solid, knotless bole of the Kauri Pine** (*Agathis australis*) **produces a first-rate timber. This specimen is estimated to be about 1000 years old, but few Kauri Pines of such great age remain in the New Zealand forests – most of them have been felled.**

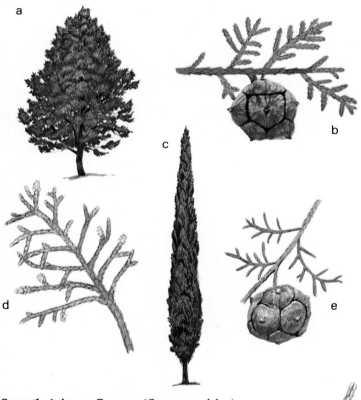

Smooth Arizona Cypress (*Cupressus glabra*): *a* **habit;** *b* **shoot with female cone.**
Italian Cypress (*Cupressus sempervirens*): *c* **habit;** *d* **shoot with male cones;** *e* **female cone.**
Western Red Cedar (*Thuja plicata*): *f* **habit;** *g* **shoot with male cones;** *h* **shoot with female cones.**

The Pine family

Arolla Pine *(Pinus cembra): a* **habit;** *b* **young shoot with winter bud;** *c* **leaves;** *d* **mature cone.**
Blue Pine *(Pinus wallichiana): e* **habit;** *f* **young shoot with winter buds;** *g* **spray of leaves;** *h* **mature cone.**

Weymouth or Eastern White Pine *(Pinus strobus): i* **habit;** *j* **shoot;** *k* **cone.**
Bristle-cone Pine *(Pinus aristata): l* **habit.**

The Pine family (Pinaceae) covers more of the earth's surface than any other tree group. Economically it is probably the most important group of trees, providing a substantial proportion of the world's insatiable desire for wood and paper products. Its ten genera contain approximately half the total number of conifer species. Unlike other conifer families, whose member species occur either as scattered individuals or in small stands, most species in the Pine family occur over large tracts of land. The family is characterized by the two seeds borne on each fertile scale in the cone.

The largest and most complex genus in the Pine family is *Pinus* itself, with about 100 species. *Pinus* species have needles in bundles or 'fascicles' of 2, 3 or 5 (rarely 1 or up to 8). Each bundle of needles is in fact a short shoot, and has a latent bud in the centre. Each short shoot is subtended by a true 'leaf' – a small triangular brown scale.

Pinus divides into two subgenera which are quite distinct in a number of ways. The soft pines belong to subgenus *Haploxylon*. The most reliable (but not most convenient) distinguishing character is that each needle contains only a single strand of vascular tissue (whereas there are two strands in the hard pines). The secondary characters are all somewhat variable. Soft pines have smooth bark (at least for a long time), cones with soft woody scales, and usually leaves in fives with deciduous sheaths at the base. The timber is high quality with very little

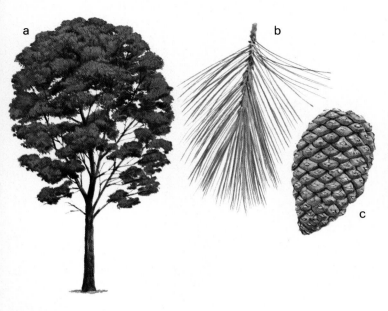

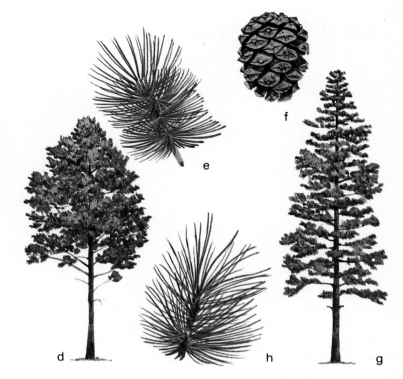

Monterey Pine *(Pinus radiata): a* **habit;**
b **leaf clusters;** *c* **cone.**
Austrian Pine *(Pinus nigra nigra): d* **habit;**
e **leafy shoot;** *f* **mature cone.**
Corsican Pine *(Pinus nigra maritima):*
g **habit;** *h* **leafy shoot.**

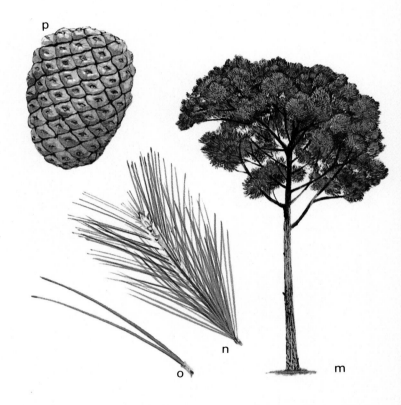

Scots Pine *(Pinus sylvestris): i* **habit;** *j* **shoot with winter buds;** *k* **leaf bundle;** *l* **mature cone.**
Stone Pine *(Pinus pinea): m* **habit;** *n* **shoot with winter bud;** *o* **leaves;** *p* **female cone.**

difference between spring and summer wood. Examples of soft pines are the Weymouth or Eastern White Pine *(Pinus strobus)* from the eastern half of North America and Mexico; Blue Pine *(P. wallichiana)* from the Himalayas, and the Arolla Pine *(P. cembra)* of central Europe. The Foxtail Pines of southwest USA are a distinctive group of three species and contain the world's oldest living thing: plants 5000 years old are still alive in the White Mountains of California. Bristlecone Pine *(P. aristata)* is the commonest species.

The hard pines usually have their needles in bundles of 2 or 3. The bark is rougher and the needles are tougher, with stomata on all three surfaces. The timber shows definite differences be-

tween spring and summer wood. Scots Pine *(P. sylvestris)* has an enormous range from the Pyrenees and northern Scotland right across the northern part of the Eurasian landmass, nearly to the shore of the Pacific Ocean in northeast China. In the upper crown the bark is orange-brown and coarsely flaky. It abruptly changes to silvery-purple and coarsely fissured, flaking in large scales to reveal red-brown below. Other hard pines are Corsican Pine *(P. nigra maritima)*, a variant of a Mediterranean Pine; Stone Pine *(P. pinea)*, a Mediterranean species; and Monterey Pine *(P. radiata)*, a three-needled pine, restricted in the wild to five limited sites in California and Mexico but planted on a vast scale in New Zealand, Chile, Australia, South Africa and Spain.

The Pine family (continued)

The remaining genera in the Pine family are distinguished by two principal characters. These are whether they have both short and long shoots or long shoots only, and whether the cone scales open to release the seeds or whether the cone disintegrates allowing seeds and cone scales to scatter.

Summary of generic characters

Genus	Short shoots	Cones
Abies	Absent	Disintegrating
Cedrus	Present	Disintegrating
Larix	Present	Opening
Picea	Absent	Opening
Pseudotsuga	Absent	Opening
Tsuga	Absent	Opening
Pinus	Present	Opening

The **Silver Firs** (*Abies*) form the second largest genus in the family, with over fifty species scattered throughout the northern hemisphere and as far south as Guatemala. European Silver Fir (*A. alba*) is the tallest-growing European tree. It

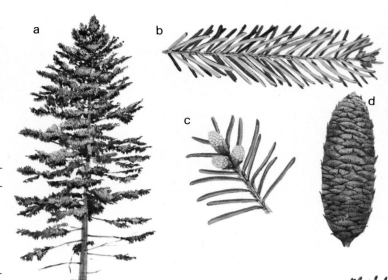

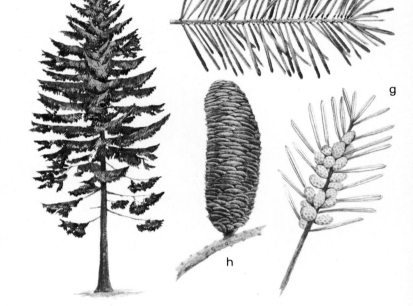

European Silver Fir (*Abies alba*): *a* **habit**; *b* **shoot**; *c* **male cones**; *d* **female cone**.
Grand Fir (*Abies grandis*): *e* **habit**; *f* **shoot**; *g* **male cones**; *h* **female cone**.

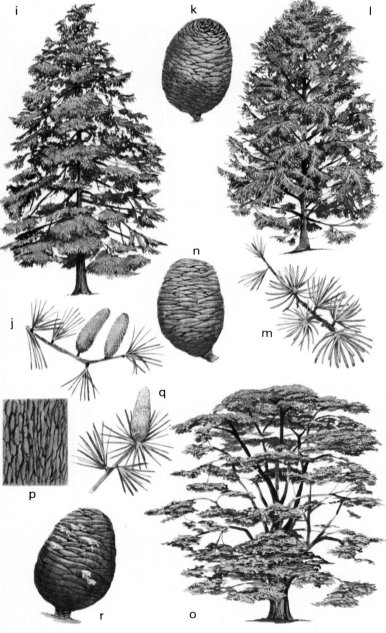

Deodar (*Cedrus deodara*): *i* **habit**; *j* **shoot with male cones**; *k* **female cone**. **Atlas Cedar** (*Cedrus atlantica*): *l* **habit**; *m* **young shoot**; *n* **female cone**. **Cedar of Lebanon** (*Cedrus libani*): *o* **habit**; *p* **bark**; *q* **male cone**; *r* **female cone**.

has a stout bole with a cracked and fissured grey bark; young trees often have blisters of resin in the bark. Grand Fir (*A. grandis*) is a taller-growing western North American species, where it is claimed to have reached 100m.

The **Cedars** (*Cedrus*) are a tight group of four species. The short shoots develop from buds on the previous year's long shoots. New rosettes of leaves appear each year for several years from each short shoot, thereafter it either dies without flowering, or flowers and then dies. The Cedar of Lebanon (*C. libani*) develops a massive bole and a crown of tiered flat branches, which are susceptible to damage by wet snow. The Atlas Cedar (*C. atlantica*), from the Atlas mountains of North Africa, has smaller cones. It is usually grown as the form *glauca* which has blue glaucous foliage. The northwest Himalayan Deodar (*C. deodara*) is the best tree, with a straight single bole.

Larches (*Larix*) are the main genus of deciduous conifers. Their soft leaves are carried on long and short shoots, but the upright cones do not break up to release

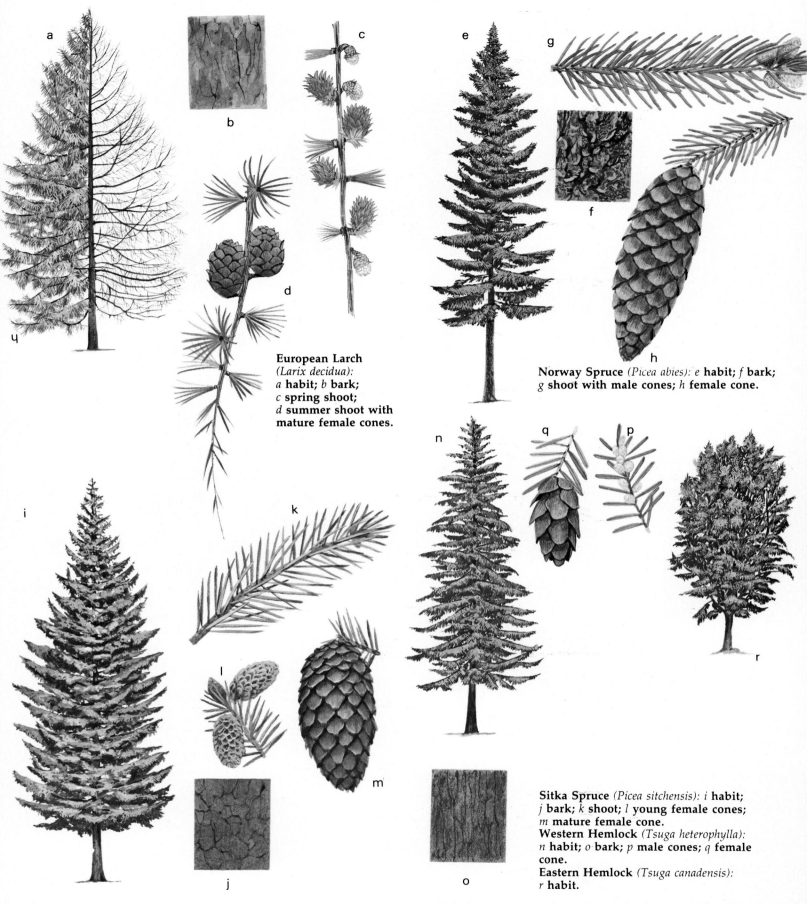

European Larch
(Larix decidua):
a **habit;** *b* **bark;**
c **spring shoot;**
d **summer shoot with
mature female cones.**

Norway Spruce *(Picea abies): e* **habit;** *f* **bark;**
g **shoot with male cones;** *h* **female cone.**

Sitka Spruce *(Picea sitchensis): i* **habit;**
j **bark;** *k* **shoot;** *l* **young female cones;**
m **mature female cone.**
Western Hemlock *(Tsuga heterophylla):*
n **habit;** *o* **bark;** *p* **male cones;** *q* **female
cone.**
Eastern Hemlock *(Tsuga canadensis):*
r **habit.**

the seeds. Only the Siberian Larch (*L. sibirica*) occupies large areas and it is the most northerly growing tree. The European Larch (*L. decidua*) and the Japanese Larch (*L. kaempferi*) are the principal species in cultivation.

The **Spruces** (*Picea*) have thirty or so species. The needles always end in a single point, either sharp or blunt, and are set on an outgrowth of a twig called a 'pulvinus'. Spruce cones are initially upright but soon bend over to hang down.

Norway Spruce (*P. abies*) is the main European species. Sitka Spruce (*P. sitchensis*) is found along the Pacific coast of North America, always within 50 miles of the sea. It is much planted in forestry.

Pseudotsuga consists of one common species from western North America and several rare ones from there and E. Asia. The genus is characterized by the curious three-pronged bract-scale of the cone. The soft foliage set straight on the shoot distinguishes it from the Spruces. Doug-

las Fir (*P. menziesii*) is an important timber tree with a red-brown heartwood.

The **Hemlocks** (*Tsuga*) are a small group closely allied to the spruces. Western Hemlock (*T. heterophylla*) is the main timber species and is another majestic western North American conifer. It has a good white timber, and is extremely tolerant of shade. As a young tree Western Hemlock can be incredibly beautiful with its nodding leading shoot and branches.

The Willow family

The Willow family (Salicaceae) contains two principal genera – *Salix*, the Willows, and *Populus*, the Poplars. Both Willows and Poplars have male and female catkins on separate trees, but a number of very convenient characters separate them.

Willows are a very wide-ranging group of plants. They are predominantly found in the cold and temperate regions of the northern hemisphere but a few species extend down South America and Africa. In size they range from minute shrublets such as *Salix herbacea*, which grows only 2–5cm high, to trees 25m tall, although most species are shrubs, especially the species used for osier production.

Willow caktins are insect-pollinated and the individual flowers each contain one or more nectar-secreting glands at their base. The male catkins are upright. Catkins are usually produced before the leaves, but there are a few exceptions, such as the Bay Willow (*S. pentandra*). The scale or bract at the base of each flower is entire. The buds have single bud scales and the winter shoots do not possess a terminal bud; growth instead recommences from axillary (side) buds near the tip.

Crack Willow (*Salix fragilis*): a **habit;** b **leafy shoot;** c **male catkins;** d **male flower;** e **female catkin.**

Sallow (*Salix caprea*): j **habit;** k **leafy shoot;** l **male catkins;** m **female catkin.**

White Willow (*Salix alba*): f **habit;** g **leafy shoot;** h **male catkins;** i **mature female catkin.**

White Poplar (*Populus alba*): n **habit;** o **leaves;** p **bark;** q **twig with male catkin;** r **male flower;** s **female catkin.**

Far left: **Aspen leaves, set on a flattened petiole, are able to flutter in the slightest breeze.**

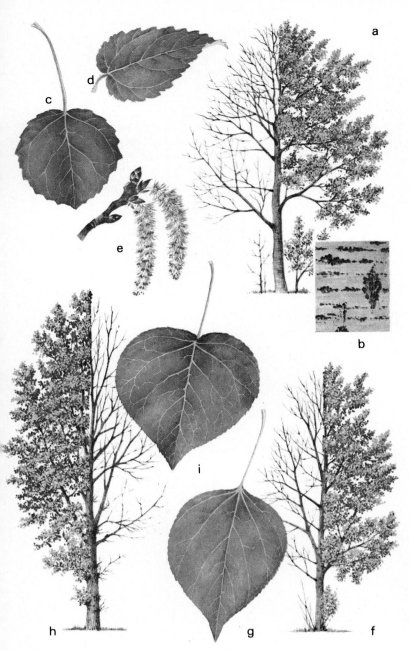

Aspen (*Populus tremula*) and White Poplar (*P. alba*) belong to a group the young bark of which is smooth and pale, becoming pitted with black diamond-shaped holes. Aspen is characterized by the round leaves set on a flattened petiole, which allows the leaf to flutter or 'quake' in the slightest breeze. White Poplar has leaves which are densely white-woolly beneath. Both produce many root suckers, as does Grey Poplar (*P.* x *canescens*), their hybrid.

Black Poplar (*P. nigra*) is normally encountered in the Lombardy Poplar form (*P. nigra 'Italica'*) or as the Manchester Poplar (*P. nigra betulifolia*). Hybrids of Black Poplar with the American *P. deltoides* are also frequently planted.

Balsam Poplars, so-called because of the sweet balsam scent they emit, have sticky or gummy winter buds which stain the fingers yellow. The leaves are oily-white in texture beneath. The commonest form in cultivation is Western Cottonwood (*P. trichocarpa*), from western North America.

Black Poplar (*Populus nigra*): *j* **habit**;
k **bark**; *l* **leaf**; *m* **fruiting catkin**; *n* **male flower**.
Hybrid Black Poplar (*Populus* x *canadensis*):
o **habit**.
Populus deltoides: *p* **habit**; *q* **bark**; *r* **leaf**;
s **male catkin**.

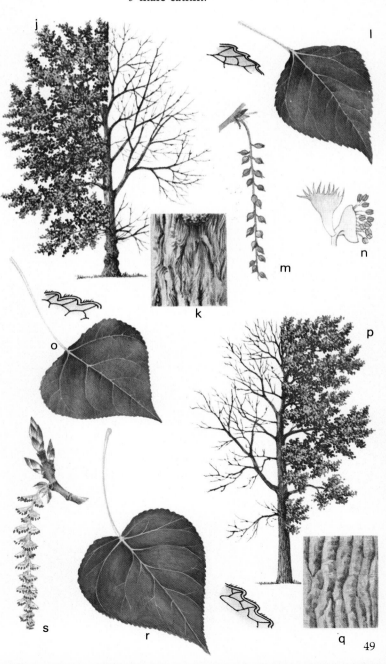

Aspen (*Populus tremula*): *a* **habit**; *b* **bark**;
c **leaf from mature tree**; *d* **leaf from sucker**;
e **male catkins**.
Balsam Poplar (*Populus balsamifera*): *f* **habit**;
g **leaf**.
Western Cottonwood (*Populus trichocarpa*):
h **habit**; *i* **leaf**.

White Willow (*Salix alba*), from Europe and West Asia, is one of the largest species. It forms an elegant tree with its narrow tapered leaves, which are permanently silky beneath. Crack Willow (*S. fragilis*) is close to White Willow but differs in its longer leaves which are soon glabrous beneath. It is called Crack Willow because the two-year-old twigs snap off cleanly at the junction if bent back. Sallow or Goat Willow (*S. caprea*) is the main tree member of the Pussy Willow group. They make trees to 10m. Bay Willow (*S. pentandra*) forms a tree to 15m. It has glossy, aromatic ovate or oval leaves which have been used as a substitute for Bay leaves.

Poplars are tall trees, most species regularly exceeding 15 or 20m. The flowers differ from Willows in that the bract beneath each flower is deeply divided, and the flowers are wind-pollinated and pendulous. The buds have many bud scales and a terminal bud is present.

The Walnut family

This family (Juglandaceae) is chiefly renowned for the nuts, which are eaten either pickled or when ripe, and for the valuable heartwood used for furniture and gunstocks. It comprises a scattered family of plants which in previous times were a major component of temperate forests. The pith in Walnut trees is not solid but divided into many small sections: Wingnuts also have this character but Hickories do not.

Walnut (*Juglans regia*) is native to southeast Europe through Asia Minor to the Himalayas and west China, and in Central Asia. It has been cultivated since ancient times in western and central Europe. The Latin name *Juglans* is based on *Jovis* and *glans*, and means Jove's nut or acorn.

Walnuts are wind-pollinated. The female flowers appear at the base of the current year's shoots as they flush in the spring. The male catkins spring from buds formed towards the end of the previous year's shoots. The leaves are pinnate and set alternately on the shoot. They are obovate in outline, with five or seven leaflets. Walnut is the only species in the genus in which the leaflets are without teeth.

Walnut fruits consist of a green outer covering over a woody-shelled nut. The green case is rich in tannin and stains the fingers yellow. The shell is sculptured and contains a single convoluted seed.

Walnuts give off a substance called Juglone which retards the growth of many plants, reducing competition. Substances like these are a form of natural 'pollution', and although they are given off by many plants, particularly those in semi-desert areas, few of those plants are trees.

Wingnut (*Pterocarya fraxinifolia*): *a* **habit;**
b **twig with leaf and female catkin.**
Walnut (*Juglans regia*): *c* **habit;** *d* **leafy twig with fruits.**
Black Walnut (*Juglans nigra*): *e* **leafy twig with fruits.**

Right: **walnut furniture. This timber has been valued by cabinet-makers for over 500 years, but is still relatively rare.**

Black Walnut *(Juglans nigra),* from eastern North America, also forms a majestic tree and is grown for its nuts and timber.

Hickories *(Carya)* are related to Walnuts and have equally delightful oily nuts. The timber is particularly good where resistance to sudden loads is needed, and it makes the best handles for tools and sports equipment. Hickories are found wild mainly in eastern North America, with four species in China; but fossils have been found throughout the northern hemisphere. Shagbark Hickory *(C. ovata)* has leaves with usually five leaflets; the terminal three are by far the largest. It has a unique bark, which exfoliates in long thin plates, remaining attached in the centre before sloughing off. This feature is only developed in trees over 25 years old. Wingnut *(Pterocarya fraxinifolia)* has small nutlets which have a wing on either side; they are carried like beads in long drooping racemes. Wingnut is native to the forests around the Caspian sea.

Rarely seen but of considerable interest is *Platycarya strobilacea.* This has upright cone-like fruits and twigs with solid pith. It was first found in 1840 as a fossil in London clay beds in the Isle of Sheppey, believed to be a million years old. Three years later the living plant was found in Japan. It also occurs in Korea, Taiwan and parts of China.

Shagbark Hickory *(Carya ovata): a* **habit;** *b* **winter twig;** *c* **flowers;** *d* **male catkins;** *e* **leaves;** *f* **fruit.**
Bitternut *(Carya cordiformis): g* **leaves;** *h* **winter twig;** *i* **fruit.**

The Birch, Alder, Hornbeam and Hazel families

Birch, Alder, Hornbeam and Hazel are often regarded as one family – Betulaceae – but are equally often divided into three families: *Betula* (Birches) and *Alnus* (Alders) remain in the Betulaceae, but *Carpinus* (Hornbeam) goes into the Carpinaceae and *Corylus* (Hazels) into the Corylaceae. These trees are all wind-pollinated and produce attractive hanging catkins. The male catkins are preformed in the summer or autumn of the previous year. In the Hornbeams they overwinter in the buds, but in the other genera they are exposed, and this provides a good identifying character.

Birches (*Betula*) are pioneer species: they will colonize suitable bare ground and quickly establish themselves. They are not long lived, and are often followed in an ecological succession by other trees which like the sheltered conditions of Birch woodland. In Arctic regions and high mountains Birch woodlands persist from generation to generation. The female catkins are erect at flowering time but soon become pendulous. At maturity they disintegrate, releasing the small winged nutlets and the bract scales which nourish the seeds.

Silver Birch (*Betula pendula*): *a* **habit;** *b* **bark;** *c* **leaf;** *d* **flowering twig with male and female catkins;** *e* **scale;** *f* **nutlet.**
Downy Birch (*Betula pubescens*): *g* **habit;** *h* **bark;** *i* **leafy twig with fruiting catkins;** *j* **scale;** *k* **nutlet.**
Paper Birch (*Betula papyrifera*): *l* **bark.**

Below: **Chinese Red-barked Birch** (*Betula albosinensis*): **This species sheds bark from the upper bark and branches in thin papery strips.**

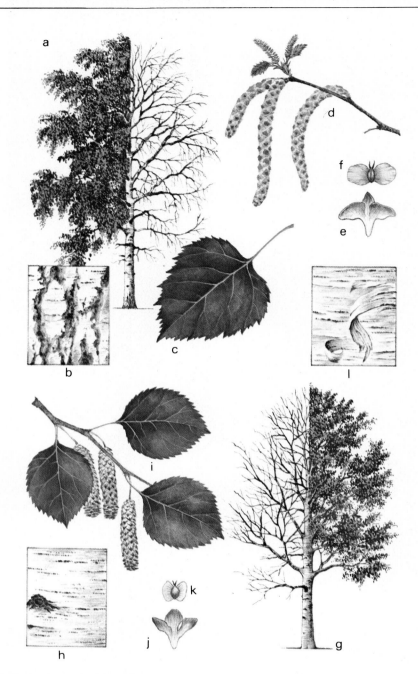

Common Alder (*Alnus glutinosa*): *m* **habit;** *n* **twig with fruiting catkins;** *o* **flowering twig with male and female catkins;** *p* **scale;** *q* **nutlet.**

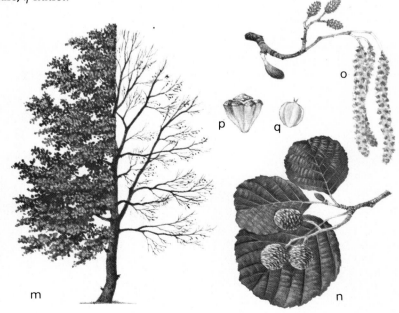

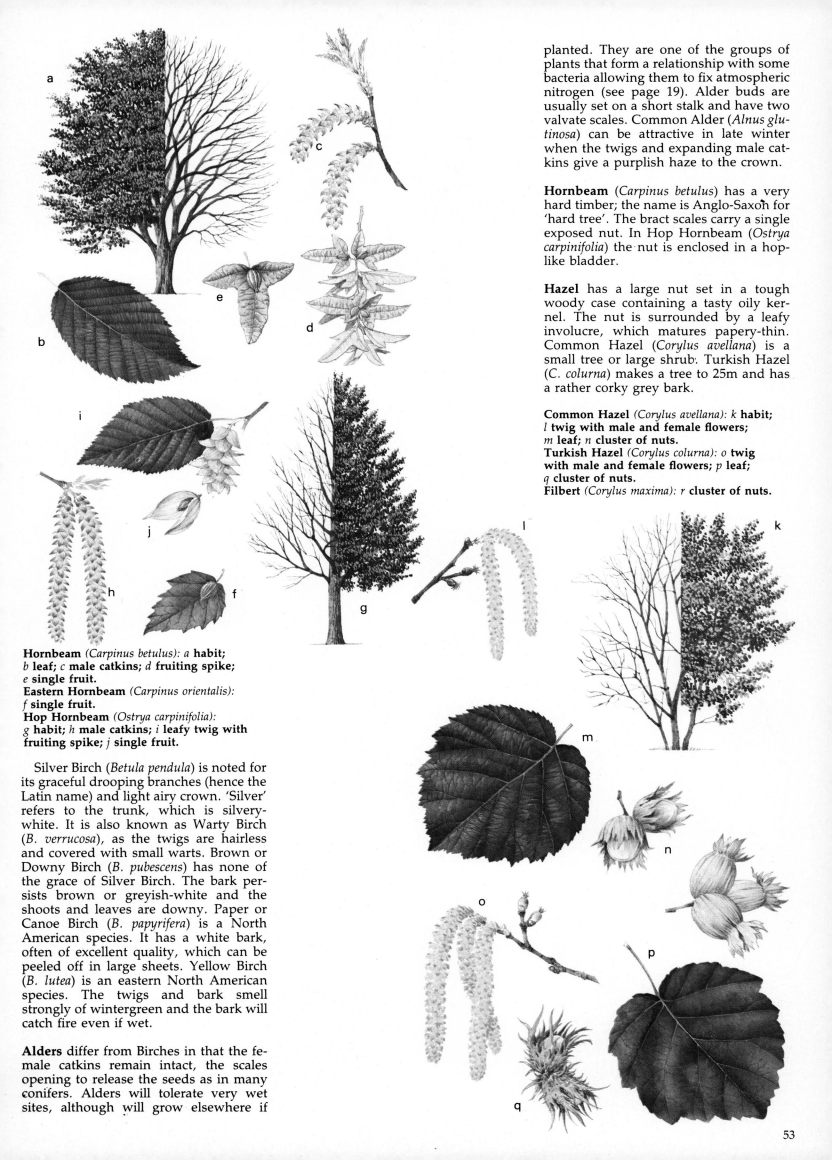

planted. They are one of the groups of plants that form a relationship with some bacteria allowing them to fix atmospheric nitrogen (see page 19). Alder buds are usually set on a short stalk and have two valvate scales. Common Alder (*Alnus glutinosa*) can be attractive in late winter when the twigs and expanding male catkins give a purplish haze to the crown.

Hornbeam (*Carpinus betulus*) has a very hard timber; the name is Anglo-Saxon for 'hard tree'. The bract scales carry a single exposed nut. In Hop Hornbeam (*Ostrya carpinifolia*) the nut is enclosed in a hop-like bladder.

Hazel has a large nut set in a tough woody case containing a tasty oily kernel. The nut is surrounded by a leafy involucre, which matures papery-thin. Common Hazel (*Corylus avellana*) is a small tree or large shrub. Turkish Hazel (*C. colurna*) makes a tree to 25m and has a rather corky grey bark.

Common Hazel (*Corylus avellana*): *k* **habit;**
l **twig with male and female flowers;**
m **leaf;** *n* **cluster of nuts.**
Turkish Hazel (*Corylus colurna*): *o* **twig with male and female flowers;** *p* **leaf;**
q **cluster of nuts.**
Filbert (*Corylus maxima*): *r* **cluster of nuts.**

Hornbeam (*Carpinus betulus*): *a* **habit;**
b **leaf;** *c* **male catkins;** *d* **fruiting spike;**
e **single fruit.**
Eastern Hornbeam (*Carpinus orientalis*):
f **single fruit.**
Hop Hornbeam (*Ostrya carpinifolia*):
g **habit;** *h* **male catkins;** *i* **leafy twig with fruiting spike;** *j* **single fruit.**

Silver Birch (*Betula pendula*) is noted for its graceful drooping branches (hence the Latin name) and light airy crown. 'Silver' refers to the trunk, which is silvery-white. It is also known as Warty Birch (*B. verrucosa*), as the twigs are hairless and covered with small warts. Brown or Downy Birch (*B. pubescens*) has none of the grace of Silver Birch. The bark persists brown or greyish-white and the shoots and leaves are downy. Paper or Canoe Birch (*B. papyrifera*) is a North American species. It has a white bark, often of excellent quality, which can be peeled off in large sheets. Yellow Birch (*B. lutea*) is an eastern North American species. The twigs and bark smell strongly of wintergreen and the bark will catch fire even if wet.

Alders differ from Birches in that the female catkins remain intact, the scales opening to release the seeds as in many conifers. Alders will tolerate very wet sites, although will grow elsewhere if

The Beech family

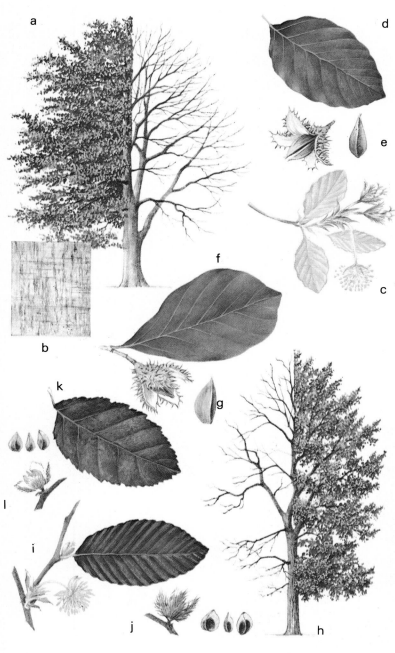

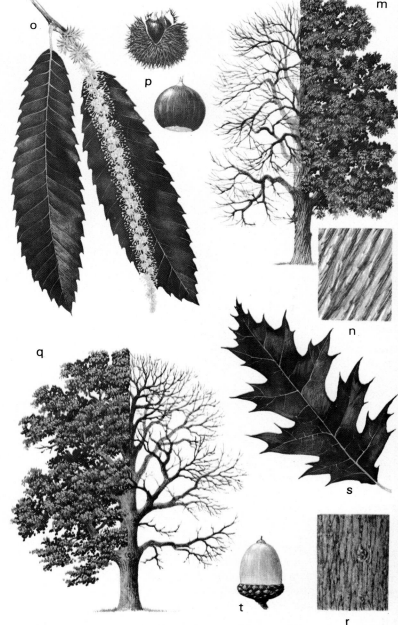

Beech (*Fagus sylvatica*): *a* **habit**; *b* **bark**; *c* **spring shoot with flowers**; *d* **mature leaf**; *e* **nuts**.
Oriental Beech (*Fagus orientalis*): *f* **leaf**; *g* **nut**.
Rauli (*Nothofagus procera*): *h* **habit**; *i* **spring shoot with flowers**; *j* **nuts**.
Roblé Beech (*Nothofagus obliqua*): *k* **leaf**; *l* **nuts**.

From the southern hemisphere come the Southern Beeches (*Nothofagus*). Many are evergreen, but Roblé Beech (*N. obliqua*) and Rauli (*N. procera*) from South America are deciduous. They are similar to Beech, particularly in the mossy cupule, but this is smaller and contains three seeds – two triangular ones and a flat central one.

Sweet Chestnut (*Castanea sativa*) has a much larger prickly fruit also containing three nuts, which are edible. It has elliptic bristle-toothed leaves, forms a big tree on a stout bole and has a distinctly spirally grained bark. The wood is easily cleft to make pales.

The **Oaks** (*Quercus*) are a large genus of over 450 species, most of which are evergreen, and half of which are found in Mexico. They are distinguished by the acorn, which sits in a cup. In Pedunculate or English Oak (*Q. robur*) the acorns are set on a long common stalk or peduncle; in Sessile Oak (*Q. petraea*) the acorns are sessile or on a short stalk. Both are important timber trees.

The Beech family (Fagaceae), which also contains the Oaks, is a large group of wind-pollinated trees which are valuable for timber; some also produce edible nuts.

Beech (*Fagus sylvatica*) is tolerant of extremely acid or strongly alkaline soils. Characteristically it has a shallow root system and demands a free-draining soil which is not compacted. The cells in the bark of most trees live for at most a few years; in Beech the cells may live for a century or more, and the bark is very thin – less than 1cm.

The brown leaves on young plants do not fall in winter, so that Beech is useful for hedging. The timber is used in furniture and for making dowels. Beech mast or fruit is carried in a mossy cup or cupule, which splits into four. Two triangular seeds occur in each cup.

Sweet Chestnut (*Castanea sativa*): *m* **habit**; *n* **bark**; *o* **leafy twig with flower spike**; *p* **fruit**.
Red Oak (*Quercus rubra*): *q* **habit**; *r* **bark**; *s* **leaf**; *t* **acorn**.

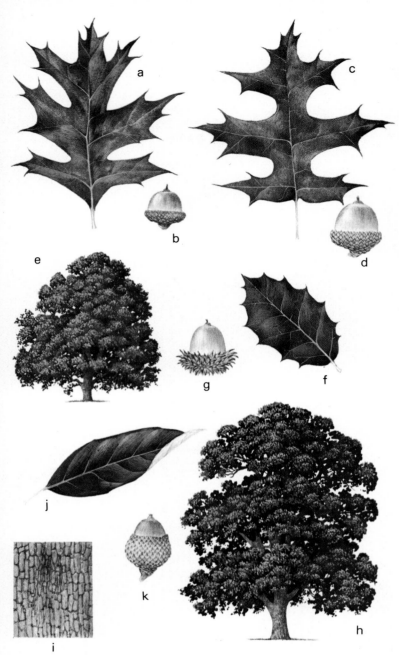

Pin Oak (*Quercus palustris*): *a* **leaf;** *b* **acorn.**
Scarlet Oak (*Quercus coccinea*): *c* **leaf;**
d **acorn.**
Quercus coccifera: *e* **habit;** *f* **leaf;**
g **acorn.**
Holm Oak (*Quercus ilex*): *h* **habit;** *i* **bark;**
j **leaf;** *k* **acorn.**

Cork Oak (*Quercus suber*): *l* **habit;** *m* **bark;**
n **leaf;** *o* **acorn.**
Turkey Oak (*Quercus cerris*): *p* **habit;** *q* **leaf;**
r **acorn.**

Sessile Oak (*Quercus petraea*): *s* **habit;**
t **leaf;** *u* **acorn.**
English Oak (*Quercus robur*): *v* **habit;**
w **bark;** *x* **leaf;**
y **acorn.**

Holm Oak (*Q. ilex*) is an evergreen species which ripens its acorn in the first autumn. Turkey Oak (*Q. cerris*) is a fast-growing Oak with clean handsome foliage but an absolutely worthless timber. Cork Oak (*Q. suber*) is related but has a thick bark from which cork is harvested. There is a hybrid between the two: *Q. x hispanica*.

Red Oaks are a large group of American Oaks. They differ in the botanically useful character of the acorn having hairs on the inside of its shell! Red Oak (*Q. rubra*), the main species encountered, has variable matt leaves and develops a large domed crown. Scarlet Oak (*Q. coccinea*) has leaves very shiny beneath, with three regular, rounded sinuses, at least along one margin. Pin Oak (*Q. palustris*) has a curious crown in which the lower branches hang down like a skirt. All three species assume rich autumn colours of red or scarlet.

The Elm and Mulberry families

The **Elms** (*Ulmus*) have suffered severely in recent years from the ravages of Dutch Elm disease and no longer occupy the prominent position they used to. Some species, and other members of the Ulmaceae, however, are tolerant of or immune to the disease. Dutch Elm disease was first noticed in northern France in 1918. At first it was put down to the effects of the lethal gases used as weapons in the First World War, but in fact it is a disease caused by a fungus, *Ceratocystis ulmi*. This grows in the spring wood and causes the blockage of the water-carrying vessels. The disease can be passed from tree to tree through root grafts – many Elm trees in fact are suckers from a common hedgerow root system – or by Elm bark beetles. Primary infections are caused by the newly emerged beetles feeding on bark or twigs in the crowns of healthy trees. If they were bred in infected bark they may introduce spores of the fungus, which can then progressively kill the tree. The name Dutch Elm disease is a tribute to the early investigations into the disease carried out by Dutch scientists.

All but three Elm species flower in early spring, before the leaves on bare branches. The flowers are followed by the green winged fruits, which appear shortly after the leaves.

Wych Elm (*Ulmus glabra*) is the only species definitely native to Britain. Smooth Elm (*U. carpinifolia*) was introduced by Belgic tribes in the first century BC. English Elm (*U. procera*) is a tall tree species which never, or very rarely, sets viable seeds.. It reproduces entirely by suckers. Japanese Elm (*U. japonica*) is one of a number of species which can show considerable tolerance to Dutch Elm disease; it is like Wych Elm in general appearance.

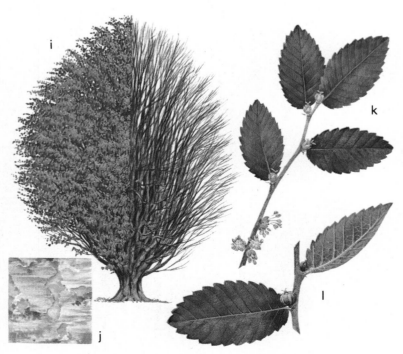

Wych Elm (*Ulmus glabra*): *a* **habit**; *b* **flowering twig;** *c* **fruit;** *d* **leafy twig.**
English Elm (*Ulmus procera*): *e* **habit;** *f* **bark;** *g* **leafy shoot;** *h* **fruit.**

Caucasian Elm (*Zelkova carpinifolia*): *i* **habit;** *j* **bark;** *k* **spring twig with flowers;** *l* **late summer twig with fruit.**

Zelkova is a related genus in which the seed is not a winged nutlet (samara) but a dry drupe (nut or nutlet surrounded by a fleshy outer covering). The Caucasian Elm (*Z. carpinifolia*) is common as a large tree but Keaki (*Z. serrata*) from Japan is more frequently planted.

Another related genus comprises the Nettle Trees (*Celtis*). These have a fleshy drupe, and the leaves always have three main veins from near the base. Southern Nettle Tree (*C. australis*) is native to southern Europe; *C. occidentalis*, from eastern N. America, is similar but its grey bark has curious narrow longitudinal ridges.

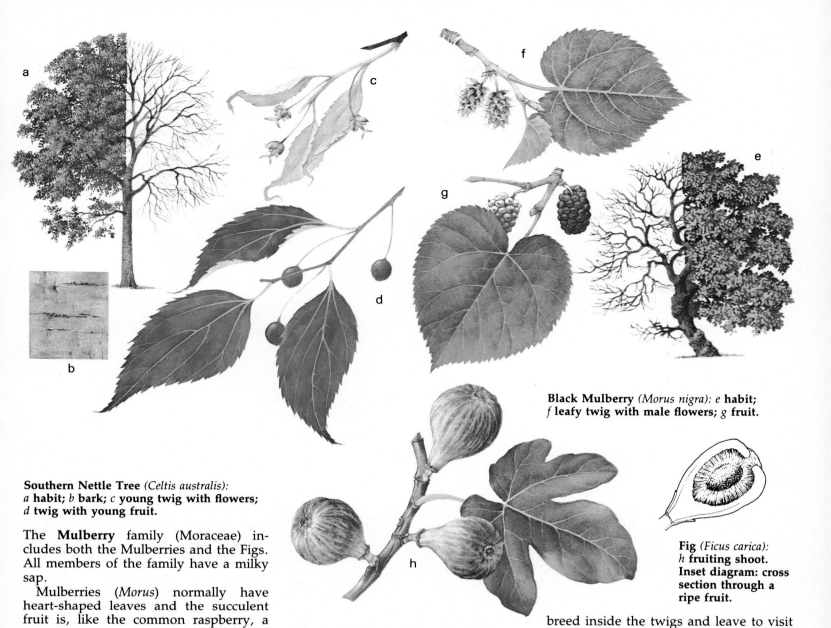

Black Mulberry *(Morus nigra): e* habit;
f leafy twig with male flowers; *g* fruit.

Fig *(Ficus carica):*
h **fruiting shoot.**
Inset diagram: cross
section through a
ripe fruit.

Southern Nettle Tree *(Celtis australis):*
a **habit;** *b* **bark;** *c* **young twig with flowers;**
d **twig with young fruit.**

The **Mulberry** family (Moraceae) includes both the Mulberries and the Figs.
All members of the family have a milky
sap.

Mulberries (*Morus*) normally have
heart-shaped leaves and the succulent
fruit is, like the common raspberry, a
syncarp – a cluster of drupes. White Mulberry (*M. alba*), the preferred food of the
silkworm, is a native of east Asia, but the
original home of Black Mulberry (*M. nigra*) is not certain. It has been so long
cultivated for its delicious tart fruit that
the original distribution is lost.

Figs are an important and mainly tropical genus of evergreen trees, but a few,
such as the Common Fig (*Ficus carica*) are
deciduous. The fruit or fig is a remarkable structure. It is a hollowed out shoot
tip, and the flower parts are inside. Pollination is achieved by special flies which

breed inside the twigs and leave to visit
the next tree by a small terminal hole.
The succulent fruit usually develops in
the second summer. Many cultivated figs
are parthenogenic, i.e. the fruits develop
without the need for fertilization, as in
northern Europe the insects do not
survive.

Elm bark beetle larvae. The beetle itself is
not the cause of Dutch Elm disease, but it
may carry spores of the fungus which is.

A commune girl stripping leaves from
White Mulberry in South China in order to
feed them to silkworms.

The Magnolia, Katsura and Laurel families

The **Magnolia** family (Magnoliaceae) is characterized by the simple structure of the flowers and fruits. The flowers do not have readily identifiable sepals and petals; the two rings of attractive parts are very similar and are collectively called 'tepals'. The fruit is a cone-like collection of spirally arranged individual carpels, each carpel containing one or two seeds.

In *Magnolia* the carpels slit open along the centre of the outer side, and the orange-red seeds fall out. For a time the seeds remain attached by thin threads. In *Liriodendron* each carpel becomes a samara, or winged nutlet, and the fruit disintegrates, releasing the seeds.

Magnolias exist in the fossil record throughout the northern hemisphere, but extant species are confined to eastern Asia and eastern North America. The Magnolia (*M. x soulangiana*) is a hybrid of two Chinese species. It is one of a number of species which produce flowers in spring on the bare branches. The flowers overwinter in large hairy buds, which are much more prominent than the leaf buds. Campbell Magnolia (*M. campbellii*) from the eastern Himalayas is a taller tree

Evergreen Magnolia or Bull Bay (*Magnolia grandiflora*): *a* **habit;** *b* **flower on leafy shoot.**
Winter's Bark (*Drimys winteri*), **a small evergreen of the Winteraceae:** *c* **flowering shoot.**

Below: the white flowers of the Hybrid Magnolia appear in profusion in spring, before the leaves are out.

a

b

and a glorious sight when laden with its 25cm flowers in spring. Cucumber Tree (*M. acuminata*) is an eastern North American species. The young fruits are like small pinky-red cucumbers; the flowers, borne after the leaves, are small, glaucous-green and yellow. Wilson Magnolia (*M. wilsonii*) is a rare tree from China. Its large fragrant white flowers are carried in early summer and hang down. Bull Bay or Evergreen Magnolia (*M. grandiflora*) is an evergreen species from southeastern USA which has large yellow-green leaves and carries its big creamy-white flowers in summer and autumn.

The Tulip Tree or Yellow Poplar (*Liriodendron tulipifera*) has flowers like those of the Cucumber Tree. The leaves are almost unique in their truncate apex and pair of side lobes. The Tulip Tree is native to eastern N. America, but an almost identical species is found in China.

Tulip Tree (*Liriodendron tulipifera*): *a* **habit;** *b* **flowering shoot.**
Sweet Bay (*Laurus nobilis*): *c* **habit;** *d* **twig with male flowers;** *e* **male flowers;** *f* **female flowers;** *g* **fruit.**
Avocado (*Persea americana*): *h* **habit;** *i* **flowering twig;** *j* **flower;** *k* **fruit.**
Katsura (*Cercidiphyllum japonicum*): *l* **habit;** *m* **leaves;** *n* **fruit.**

Katsura (*Cercidiphyllum japonicum*), from Japan and China, is in its own family, the Cercidiphyllaceae; it assumes brilliant autumn colours of fiery or pastel hues. The young fresh green leaves are also attractive when displayed on the arching branches in spring.

The **Laurel** family (Lauraceae) is a vast assemblage of mainly tropical or subtropical plants. The plants contain aromatic oils and a sniff of crushed foliage is usually a delight. However, over indulgence in the fine aroma of the Headache Tree (*Umbellularia californica*) repays with a splitting headache after one or two hours. Bay Laurel (*Laurus nobilis*), a native of the Mediterranean region, provides the Bay leaves used in cooking and once supplied the wreaths given to victors and poets in Roman times. Poets received fruiting wreaths, and apart from the title 'Poet Laureate' this ancient practice has given us the term 'bachelor' as applied to recipients of degrees, via the French *bachelier*, from 'baccalaureus' or Laurel berry.

Avocado (*Persea americana*) is a tropical member of the family. It is native to Central America but widely cultivated for its fruit.

The Legume family

The Leguminosae is one of the largest and most important families of plants. It contains approximately 500 genera and 15,000 species, although this includes many herbs. It is sometimes considered as three separate families – Mimosaceae, Caesalpinaceae and Papilionaceae (Fabaceae).

The feature common to all members of the Leguminosae is the fruit or 'legume'. This is a flattened pod-like structure the two halves of which split when ripe: alternate seeds are attached to the top of each half. The usual legume or pea-type flower has five petals. The top petal, called the 'standard', covers the others in bud. The two side petals are called the 'wings' and the lower two are hooked together to make the 'keel'.

Members of the legume family support nitrogen-fixing bacteria in nodules on their roots. They are able to convert or 'fix' atmospheric nitrogen to make the nitrogen compounds used in plant and animal cells, and this boosts the growth of the plant (see page 19).

The Judas Tree (Cercis siliquastrum), a native of the eastern Mediterranean, is an atypical legume. Most legumes have pinnate or doubly pinnate (bipinnate) leaves, but in Judas Tree they are simple and rounded, although some are notched at the apex. Judas Tree also produces flowers on old wood, not just on the current or previous year's twigs. Carob or Locust Tree (Ceratonia siliqua) also flowers on old wood but its leaves have two to five pairs of leaflets without a terminal one. The seeds formed the original 'carat' weight, while its sweet brown pods were the 'locusts' eaten by John the Baptist.

Honey Locust (Gleditsia triacanthos) has foliage which is either pinnate with 14–36 leaflets, or bipinnate with 8–14 pinnae, each with about 20 pinnules, or little leaflets. The flowers do not have the true pea-like arrangement of petals. They are followed by spirally twisted pods up to 45 cm long, which contain a sugary pulp. Honey Locust, from eastern North America, has clusters of fierce three-pointed spines on the black-barked bole and branches. Robinia or Black Locust (Robinia pseudacacia), also from eastern North America, has two short curved spines beside each bud on the vigorous shoots. The leaves are pinnate and hide the buds in the base of petiole. Its white flowers are followed by short dry pods. Laburnum (Laburnum anagyroides and L. alpinum) has trifoliate leaves (i.e. with three leaflets). The racemes of yellow flowers are an attractive sight in early summer. The seeds are poisonous as with many legumes (including certain beans if not properly cooked). The pods are constricted between the seeds. Wisteria (Wisteria sinensis) is a woody legume which is a climbing plant.

Judas Tree (Cercis siliquastrum): a **habit**; b **flowering twig**; c **fruiting twig**.
Carob or Locust Tree (Ceratonia siliqua): d **habit**; e **flowering twig**; f **male flower**; g **immature fruit**.
Honey Locust (Gleditsia triacanthos): h **habit**; i **detail of bole**; j **flowering twig**; k **flower**; l **fruit**.

Robinia or Black Locust (Robinia pseudacacia): m **habit**; n **flowering twig**; o **pods**.

Acacia species are the principal constituents of tree cover in hot dry areas. They are particularly a feature of the savannas of Africa and Australia. The appeal of their flowers is in the massed boss of stamens, and their twigs usually carry large thorns. All species have bipinnate foliage but in a number this only occurs on juvenile plants. In older trees 'phyllodes' (green leaflike structures) develop out of the petiole and are carried instead of leaves.

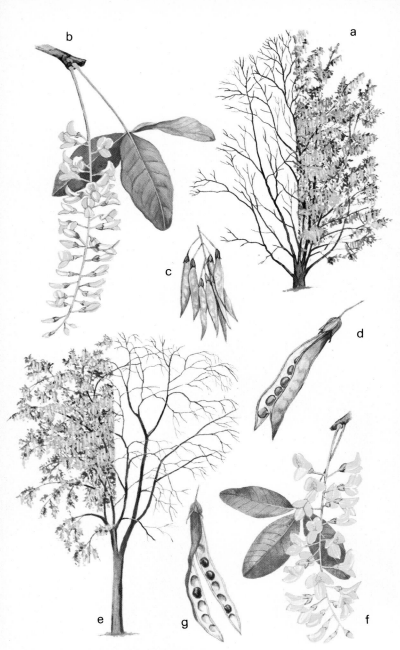

Alpine or Scotch Laburnum (*Laburnum alpinum*): *a* **habit;** *b* **flowering twig;** *c* **fruit cluster;** *d* **ripe fruit.**
Common Laburnum (*Laburnum anagyroides*): *e* **habit;** *f* **flowering twig;** *g* **ripe fruit.**

Silver Wattle or Mimosa (*Acacia dealbata*): *h* **habit;** *i* **bark;** *j* **leaf** *k* **flowers;** *l* **legume.**

Above: many of the African acacias are armed with long sharp thorns; this specimen also bears parasitic galls.

Blackwood (*Acacia melanoxylon*): *m* **habit;** *n* **phyllodes with inflorescence;** *o* **legume.**

The Rose family

The Rose family (Rosaceae) consists of four divisions but only two contain trees, and these are rarely more than 15m tall. These are the Prunoideae, centered on the cherries (*Prunus*) and the Pomoideae, which includes the apples (*Malus*).

Cherries (*Prunus*) are the only tree genus in the **Prunoideae**. The fruit is a drupe, a fleshy-coated fruit which does not open and which contains a hard bony seed. The genus contains a number of different species groupings. The Cherries typified by the Gean or Wild Cherry (*P. avium*) have the flowers in umbels appearing with or slightly in advance of the leaves. Bird Cherry (*P. padus*) has its flowers and fruits in a leafy raceme. It is native right across the Eurasian landmass, from Scotland to Manchuria. Cherry Laurel (*P. laurocerasus*) and Portuguese Laurel (*P. lusitanica*) both have evergreen leaves; the flowers and fruit are like Bird Cherry but the peduncle is not leafy. In the almond/plum/apricot part of *Prunus* the fruit is grooved and the trees usually flower on bare branches. In the Plums, such as Myrobalan (*P. cerasifera*) and Sloe (*P. spinosa*) the fruits are covered with a waxy bloom. In Apricot (*P. armeniaca*) the flowers are sessile, fruits are hairy and the twigs lack terminal buds. Almond (*P. dulcis*) and Peach (*P. persica*) fruits are hairy and the stones pitted and grooved.

The Pomoideae are characterized by the fruit, which is a pome (i.e. a fleshy apple-like structure). The Pomoideae contain a number of closely related genera, which hybridize fairly readily.

In the Common Hawthorn or Quickthorn (*Crataegus monogyna*) the fruit contains a single nutlet surrounded by a thin flesh. Midland Hawthorn (*C. oxycantha*) has haws with two nuts, while other species contain up to five. *Cotoneaster* dif-

Common Hawthorn or Quickthorn (*Crataegus monogyna*): *i* **habit**; *j* **flowering shoot**; *k* **fruit**.

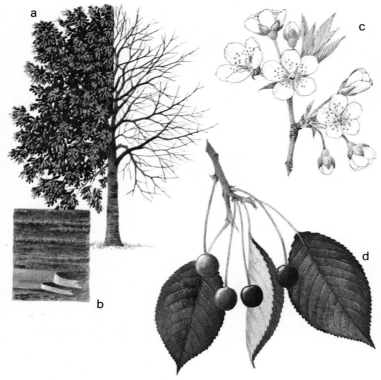

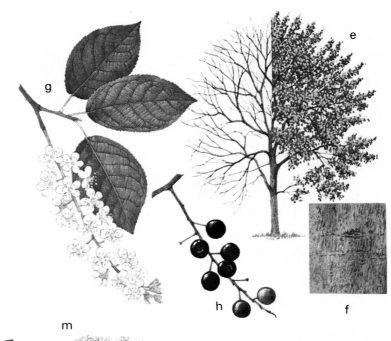

Gean (*Prunus avium*): *a* **habit**; *b* **bark**; *c* **flowers**; *d* **leafy twig with fruits**. **Bird Cherry** (*Prunus padus*): *e* **habit**; *f* **bark**; *g* **leafy twig with flowers**; *h* **fruits**.

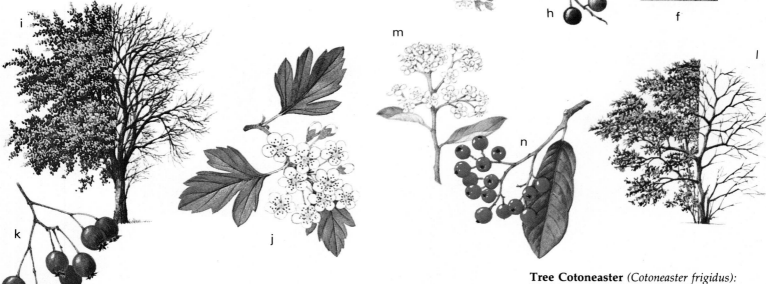

Tree Cotoneaster (*Cotoneaster frigidus*): *l* **habit**; *m* **flowering twig**; *n* **fruit**.

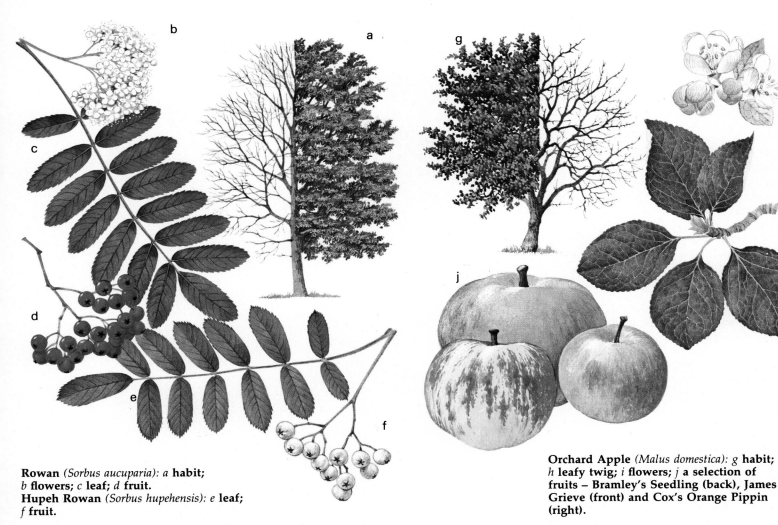

Rowan *(Sorbus aucuparia):* a **habit;**
b **flowers;** c **leaf;** d **fruit.**
Hupeh Rowan *(Sorbus hupehensis):* e **leaf;**
f **fruit.**

Orchard Apple *(Malus domestica):* g **habit;**
h **leafy twig;** i **flowers;** j **a selection of**
fruits – Bramley's Seedling (back), James
Grieve (front) and Cox's Orange Pippin
(right).

fers from Common Hawthorn in that the leaves are entire, not toothed or lobed, and the trees are without spines. Tree Cotoneaster (*C. frigidus*) is a Himalayan species which is semi-evergreen and may reach 15m.

The genus *Sorbus* includes both the Rowans (or Mountain Ashes) and the Whitebeams. Rowan (*S. aucuparia*) has scarlet berries which turn in midsummer and are quickly devoured by birds; Hupeh Rowan (*S. hupehensis*) has white ber-

ries which may last nearly until Easter. Whitebeams (*S. aria*) have simple, toothed leaves. They are initially covered with a silvery-white down but this only persists on the lower surface. Wild Service Tree (*S. domestica*) is superficially similar to Rowan but the flowers are botanically different. The fruit is large (up to 2cm).

Apples (*Malus*) differ from *Sorbus* in that the flowers are in umbel-like racemes instead of compound corymbs.

The Orchard Apple (*M. domestica*) is a complex hybrid species selected for its fruit. Japanese Crab (*M. floribunda*) and Siberian Crab (*M. baccata*) are two ornamental species with showy flowers and small fruits. Pears (*Pyrus*) differ from apples in floral and fruit details. The fruit is often if not always pear-shaped and contains many grit-cells. Pear (*P. communis*) is a hybrid species selected for its large fruit. Willow-leaf Pear (*P. salicifolia*) has greyish willow-like foliage.

Whitebeam *(Sorbus aria):* k **habit;**
l **flowering twig;**
m **fruit.**

Pear *(Pyrus communis):* n **habit;**
o **flowering twig;**
p **fruiting twig.**

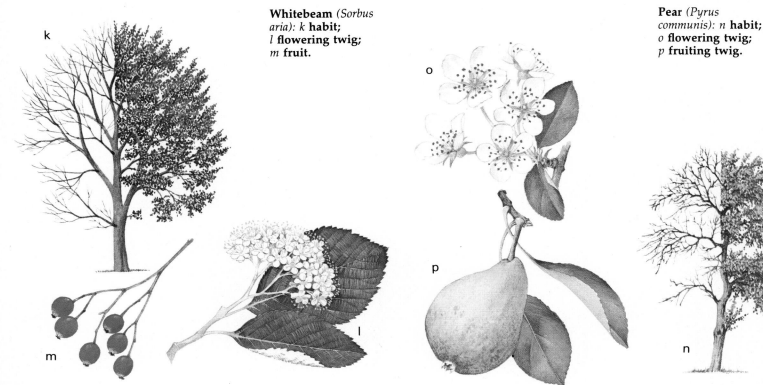

The Citrus Fruit family

The Citrus Fruit family (Rutaceae) is of considerable economic importance as it contains the Citrus fruits; other members of the family are of passing interest and only one is of particular value for providing timber. The Rutaceae are found in tropical and warm temperate regions, with 150 genera and over 1000 species. The main diagnostic feature of the family is the presence of black dots on the leaves: these are oil-producing glands which give the crushed foliage a rich Citrus scent. All the Citrus fruits form small trees up to 10m tall, and are evergreen. They are native to eastern Asia, particularly China.

In *Citrus* the fruit is the well known orange, lemon or grapefruit. It is a juicy berry, divided into a dozen or so segments with seeds in each segment, although for commercial plantations seedless plants have been selected. The fruit is enclosed by a thick skin in two layers – one pithy and white, the other leathery, coloured and rich in oil-bearing glands. Apart from the industry based upon the fleshy part of the fruit, natural oils are distilled from the outer skin and used in perfumery, and to flavour Earl Grey's tea.

Lemon (*Citrus limon*) carries the distinctive lemon fruit. The flowers, which are often found together with the fruits on this and other *Citrus* species, are white and delightfully fragrant, with five petals. Lemon leaves appear to have a curious joint part way along: the true leaf-blade is the portion above the joint, that below is the petiole, which is frequently winged. Lemon also has spiny shoots, the spines being modified leaves.

Sweet Orange (*C. sinensis*), Grapefruit (*C. paradisi*) and Lime (*C. aurantifolia*) differ mainly in their fruits. Mandarin, Tangerine or Satsuma (*C. reticulata*) has a soft loose orange skin.

The Japanese *Poncirus trifoliata* is close to *Citrus* but it has deciduous trifoliate leaves on a winged petiole. It is very thorny and hardy, even ripening its bitter fruit in England. It is often used as a rootstock for grafting *Citrus* trees.

The genus *Zanthoxylum* is a large mainly tropical one, although a few species are hardy. The fruit opens by two valves to release the single black seed. Seeds of the Toothache Tree or Prickly Ash (*Z. americanum*) may be chewed to alleviate dental discomfort. Euodia (*Euodia daniellii*) has a similar fruit and it flowers in the autumn when few other trees are in flower. Amur Cork Tree (*Phellodendron amurense*) has a corky bark but lacks the black dots in the foliage characteristic of the family. Both are deciduous and from northeast Asia.

Hop Tree (*Ptelea trifoliata*) is a small deciduous tree from eastern North America. The generic name *Ptelea* is the Greek for Elm and refers to the Elm-like fruit.

Sweet Orange (*Citrus sinensis*): *a* **habit;** *b* **flowering twig;** *c* **fruit.**
Lemon (*Citrus limon*): *d* **habit;** *e* **flowering twig;** *f* **fruit.**
The fruits of *g Citrus aurantium;* *h Citrus bergamia;* *i Citrus deliciosa;* *j Citrus paradisi;* *k Citrus grandis;* *l Citrus limetta;* *m Citrus medica.*

Opposite: **Orange and olive trees growing together in a Spanish grove.**

Below: **Cross-section through a cultivated orange.**

The Myrtle and Protea families

The **Myrtles** (Myrtaceae) are a large family of perhaps 3000 species, mainly concentrated in the continents of the southern hemisphere. They are all woody evergreen species, ranging from the tallest hardwoods to scrubby shrubs.

Myrtus includes one European species amongst its 200. This is Common Myrtle (*M. communis*) which forms a shrub or small tree to 5m high. It has opposite leathery leaves which, like in the rest of the family, are dotted with glands, as are the shoots and flowering parts. The solitary fragrant flowers are borne in summer and are followed by the purplish-black berries in the autumn. Orange-bark Myrtle (*M. luma*) is a native of the temperate forests of S. America. It forms a tree to 20m and its main feature is the flaking cinnamon-brown bark.

Eucalyptus is the most commonly encountered genus. It consists of some six hundred species, nearly all confined to Australia. They include the tallest hardwoods in the world, with *E. regnans* exceeding 100m in Tasmania. They have been extensively planted throughout the tropical and temperate parts of the world as they are capable of extremely fast growth.

Eucalypts are characterized by a number of features. The flower buds are formed during the summer before they open. The petals are fused together into a cap, called an operculum, which covers the top of the bud and falls away when

Red Gum (*Eucalyptus camaldulensis*):
a **habit**; *b* **bark**; *c* **juvenile leaves**; *d* **mature leaves**; *e* **inflorescence in bud**; *f* **fruit.**
Blue Gum (*Eucalyptus globulus*): *g* **habit;** *h* **bark**; *i* **juvenile leaves**; *j* **flowering twig;** *k* **fruit.**

Right: **profuse regrowth of branches along the trunk of** *Eucalyptus mitida* **in Cornwall following the death of the crown from extreme cold in the winter of 1978.**

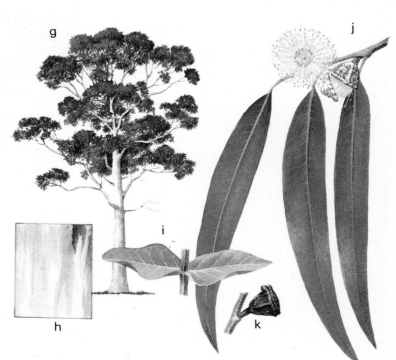

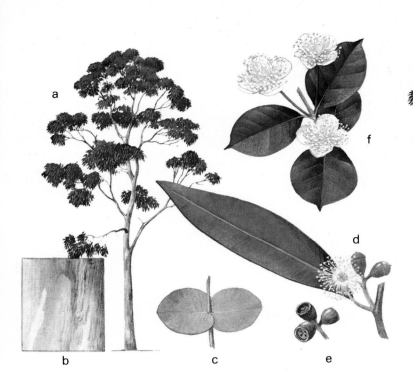

Cider Gum (*Eucalyptus gunnii*): *a* **habit;** *b* **bark;** *c* **juvenile leaves;** *d* **flowering twig;** *e* **fruit.**
Orange-bark Myrtle (*Myrtus luma*): *f* **flower.**
Chilean Fire Bush (*Embothrium coccineum*): *g* **habit;** *h* **flower.**

the flowers open. The fruit is somewhat urn-shaped and the seeds are released through slits across the flattened top.

Eucalypts produce five different types of leaves – cotyledons, seedling leaves, juvenile leaves, intermediate leaves and adult leaves. Juvenile leaves are produced whenever a mature tree is cut back, but Eucalypts have a remarkable capacity to make new growth, either from dormant meristem tissue or from lignotubers – woody knobbles formed at ground-level and designed to survive a passing fire.

Right: many species of Eucalypt have brilliant distinctive flowers. In bud the petals are fused together into a cap, or 'operculum', which falls away when the flowers open.

Cider Gum (*E. gunnii*) is one of the hardiest species, and cider can be made from the sap. Blue Gum (*E. globulus*) is a fast-growing tree used for timber in warm temperate climates and as a summer bedding plant in Britain. It has long sickle-shaped leaves and large single bloomed capsules. Red Gum (*E. camaldulensis*) was first described from trees introduced to Italy, although it is widespread in Australia. The fruit has four curved triangular valves.

Eucalypts provide timber but also contain many unique oils, which are distilled from the leaves. Cloves are the flower buds of *Syzyium aromaticum* while Guava (*Psidium guajava*) is a Central American species with an edible fruit.

The **Protea** family (Proteaceae) is a southern hemisphere family of over 1000 species of trees and shrubs, all with alternate leaves.

Banksia has vast flower heads, containing up to 1000 flowers. Chilean Fire Bush (*Embothrium coccineum*) has flamboyant flowers in early summer. It is a hardy narrow-columnar evergreen tree. Waratah (*Telopea truncata*), the Tasmanian national flower, is a similar but smaller tree without the fiery sparkle of *Embothrium*. Both have heads of 20–30 tubular scarlet flowers.

The Lime, Maple, Plane and Horse Chestnut families

The **Lime** or **Linden** family (Tiliaceae) is a group of mainly tropical trees and shrubs. The principal tree genus is Lime or Linden (*Tilia*) and this is found predominantly in temperate parts of the northern hemisphere. The flowers, which are richly scented, are subtended by a large leafy bract of which the basal end is fused to the peduncle. The fruit is a nutlet.

Small-leafed Lime (*Tilia cordata*) and Large-leafed Lime (*T. platyphyllos*) are the tallest broadleaved trees in Europe, the latter attaining 45m. They are atypical of Limes in that the hairs on the leaves are all simple, whereas most Limes have branched or fascicled hairs. In Silver Lime (*T. tomentosa*) the hairs are star-shaped and closely pressed on the leaf underside. Common Lime (*T.* x *europaea*) is a hybrid between the Small and Large-leafed Limes. It is a poor reflection of its parents, having abundant suckers on the bole and being much troubled by sap-sucking aphids which secrete 'honeydew' – a sticky sugary solution.

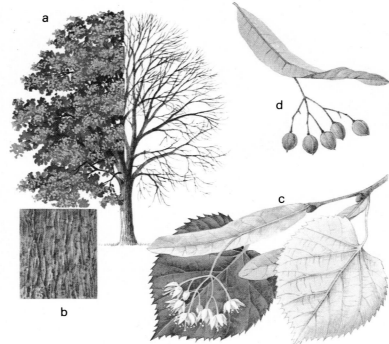

Silver Lime (*Tilia tomentosa*): *a* **habit;** *b* **bark;** *c* **flowering shoot;** *d* **fruit.**
Large-leafed Lime (*Tilia platyphyllos*): *e* **habit;** *f* **bark;** *g* **leaf;** *h* **flowers;** *i* **fruit.**
Small-leafed Lime (*Tilia cordata*): *j* **habit;** *k* **flowering shoot;** *l* **fruit.**
Norway Maple (*Acer platanoides*): *m* **habit;** *n* **flowering twig;** *o* **leaf;** *p* **young fruits.**
Sycamore (*Acer pseudoplatanus*): *q* **habit;** *r* **flowering twig;** *s* **fruits.**

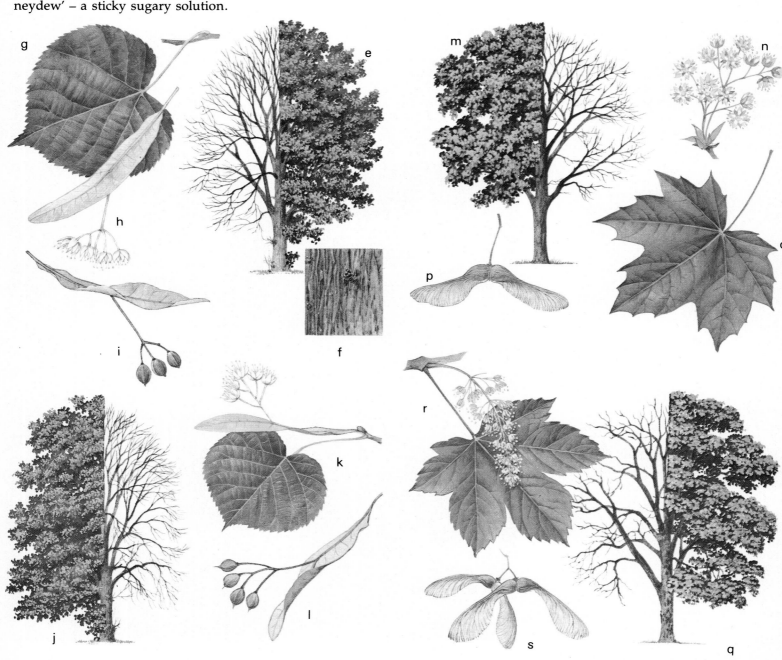

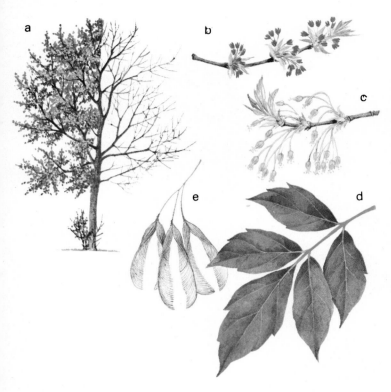

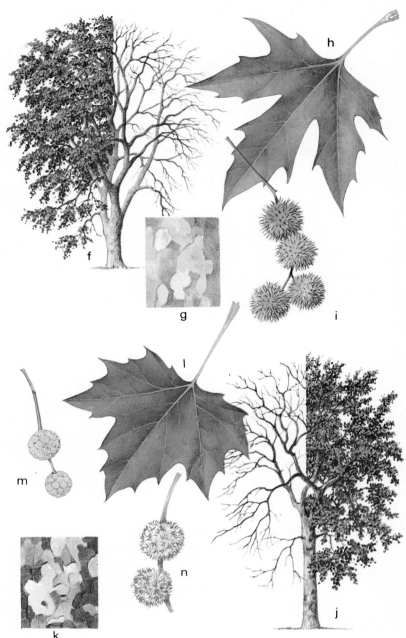

The **Maple** family (Aceraceae) consists of only one small genus in addition to *Acer*, the widespread Maples. Sycamore (*Acer pseudoplatanus*) is a west Asian and European species which produces a fine veneer timber. Norway Maple (*A. platanoides*) has a similar distribution to Sycamore. The leaves have entire lobes with teeth on the shoulders, and turn golden in autumn. The sap in the leaf stalk is milky. Box Elder (*A. negundo*) is an American species. It has been tapped to give maple syrup, but this is mainly obtained from the Sugar Maple (*A. saccharum*), which has leaves like Norways but without the milky sap.

The **Plane** family (Platanaceae) is a small group of about ten species. The principal member is the London Plane (*Platanus x acerifolia*) which is a hybrid between Oriental Plane (*P. orientalis*) from the E. Mediterranean, and the American Sycamore or Buttonwood (*P. occidentalis*).

The Planes differ from the Maples in that they have alternate leaves, and the conical winter buds are hidden in the base of the petiole. The fruit is a globular cluster of seeds carried hanging in groups of 2–4. Nearly all parts of the Plane are covered with stellate hairs.

The **Horse Chestnut** family (Hippocastanaceae) is a small group from temperate regions of the northern hemisphere and tropical Central America. The large palmately compound leaves, set in pairs on stout shoots, and the leathery fruit containing one or occasionally more large seeds, distinguish the principal genus, *Aesculus*. The Horse Chestnut (*A. hippocastanum*) is a rare native of the Balkans. It has large resinous winter buds and spiny fruit. The seed or 'conker' is a rich chestnut-brown with a large pale brown 'hilum' or scar.

Box Elder (*Acer negundo*): *a* **habit**; *b* **male flowers**; *c* **female flowers**; *d* **leaf**; *e* **fruit**.

Oriental Plane (*Platanus orientalis*): *f* **habit**; *g* **bark**; *h* **leaf**; *i* **fruiting heads**.
London Plane (*Platanus x hispanica*): *j* **habit**; *k* **bark**; *l* **leaf**; *m* **male catkins**; *n* **female catkins**.

Horse Chestnut (*Aesculus hippocastanum*): *o* **habit**; *p* **leaf**; *q* **flower**; *r* **fruit and seed**.

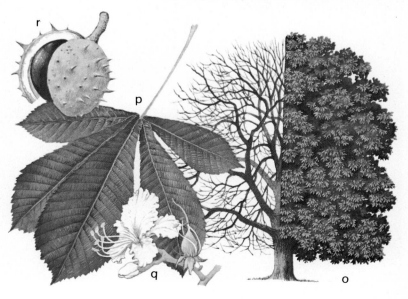

The Olive and Persimmon families

The **Olive** or **Ash** family (Oleaceae) is cosmopolitan in distribution, with species in all six continents. It consists of two subfamilies centred around *Olea*, consisting of trees and shrubs, and *Jasminum*, including few trees but many shrubs and climbers. The family takes its name from *Olea*, the Olives. This genus is found only in tropical and warm temperate parts of the old world. The Olive (*Olea europaea*) is of considerable commercial importance, and is extensively planted throughout the Mediterranean region. Its native zone has been masked, but was probably southwest Asia.

The Privets (*Ligustrum*) are mainly known as hedging shrubs but include a few attractive small trees. Chinese Privet (*L. lucidum*) is an excellent evergreen tree capable of reaching 15m or more; it has glossy leaves and it flowers in late summer.

In the Ashes (*Fraxinus*) the fruit is a samara, or winged nutlet. Common Ash (*F. excelsior*) belongs to a section of the genus in which the flowers are carried on the naked branches in spring, before the leaves, and are without petals or sepals. It also has black buds and pale grey bark with inter-leafing ridges. Narrow-leaf Ash (*F. angustifolia*) has a dark grey, almost blackish bark, and is native to the eastern half of the Mediterranean. Manna Ash (*F. ornus*) from S. Europe and W. Asia belongs to a different part of the genus. The bark is smooth and dark grey, whilst the buds are grey-brown. Manna sugar is produced following damage to the bark, and can be harvested from incisions in the stem.

Chinese Privet *(Ligustrum lucidum):* a **habit;** b **flowering twig;** c **flower;** d **fruit.**
Olive *(Olea europaea):* e **habit;** f **flowering twig;** g **flower;** h **fruit.**

Left: **pickers collecting a harvest of black olives on the island of Corfu.**

The **Persimmon** family (Ebenaceae) consists of the widely distributed genus *Diospyros* with some 400–500 species (half in Malaysia), and a second, insignificant genus. *Diospyros* is important as the source of ebony, a hard, fine-grained and valuable black timber, which is obtained from several of the large tree species, especially *D. ebenum* from Sri Lanka and *D. reticulata* from Mauritius. The trees also yield economically important fruits – persimmon and the date plum. These are large berries containing several seeds; the flesh is very astringent until the fruit is fully ripe.

Diospyros species have a strongly monopodial growth habit, i.e. with a strong central leader and rather horizontal branching. The bark is characteristically and rather curiously broken into small black squares. Date Plum (*D. lotus*) has a wide distribution from Asia Minor to China, although it is possible that its range has been confused by ancient introductions. The fruits are small. Persimmon or Kaki (*D. kaki*) is a Chinese species which is extensively cultivated for the large fruits. In some forms these are constricted around the middle like a cottage loaf.

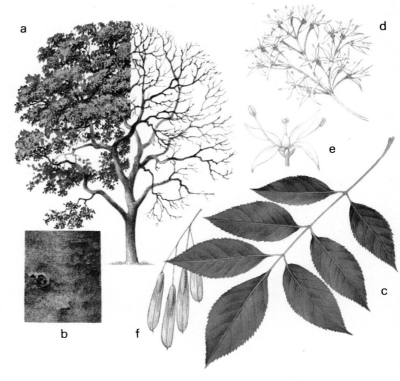

Manna Ash (*Fraxinus ornus*): *a* **habit**; *b* **bark**; *c* **leaf**; *d* **part of inflorescence**; *e* **flower**; *f* **fruits**.

Date Plum (*Diospyros lotus*): *r* **habit**; *s* **leaf with female flower**; *t* **fruit**.
Persimmon or Kaki (*Diospyros kaki*): *u* **habit**; *v* **leaf with male flowers**; *w* **immature fruit**.

Common Ash (*Fraxinus excelsior*): *g* **habit**; *h* **bark**; *i* **flowering twig**; *j* **male flower**; *k* **leaf**; *l* **fruits**.
Narrow-leaf Ash (*Fraxinus angustifolia*): *m* **habit**; *n* **bark**; *o* **flowering twig**; *p* **leaf**; *q* **fruits**.

The Palm family

The **Palm** family (Palmae) is a primitive group of plants which are nearly exclusively tropical or warm temperate in distribution. Half of the 2800 species occur in the Far East, with fewer in the Americas and Africa and only two species in Europe.

Palms are members of the monocotyledons, an important group of plants best known for grasses, bulbs such as Daffodils, and Orchids.

They are mainly trees, but a number are shrubs and a few are even climbing plants. Palms are odd in having only a single growing point or bud, and they do not have the capacity to develop additional buds. If their single bud is destroyed or damaged the entire plant will wither and die. There are only a handful of exceptions to this and these have primitive dichotomous or forked branching.

Monocotyledons do not possess the capacity to develop further woody tissues after the stem is made. In gymnosperms and dicotyledonous plants the twig or stem is formed of primary woody tissues, and then each year a new layer of secondary water-conducting tissues is added. Palms have to lay down all their woody tissue at the first go. This presents a problem for the seedling which is destined to form a 15–25m tree, starting from a seed as small as a date stone. Before height growth is commenced the seedling must develop a base as broad as the eventual stem.

Below: **fruits of the Oil Palm** (*Elais guineensis*), **from which palm oil is obtained.**

Chusan Palm
(*Trachycarpus fortunei*):
a **habit;** *b* **leaf;**
c **inflorescence.**
Date Palm (*Phoenix dactylifera*): *d* **habit;**
e **leaf;** *f* **cluster of fruits;** *g* **single fruit.**

Germination of the seed of Coconut Palm (*Cocos nucifera*).

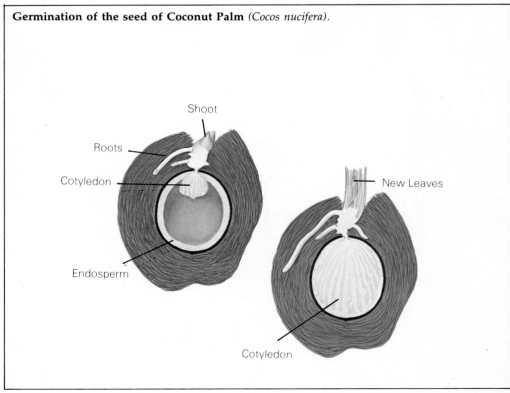

The wood of Palm species is composed of bundles of vascular tissue set in woody packing cells. The bundles may be evenly spread, but when they are concentrated around the perimeter extremely tough hard wood is formed. This may be used as timber.

Palms only have leaves below the terminal bud, and these may be pinnate or fan-shaped. Many Palms flower intermittently over many years from lateral inflorescences, but a number of species are monocarpic: in these the inflorescence is terminal and the plant dies after one strenuous burst of flowering, utilizing starch stored over several seasons in the stem. The floral parts are in threes, and in some species the inflorescences are very complex, with up to 250,000 flowers.

Palms yield a number of desirable products. Dates are obtained from the Date Palm (*Phoenix dactylifera*) and coconuts, copra and coir from the Coconut Palm (*Cocos nucifera*). Palm oil is obtained from the fruits of the Oil Palm (*Elaeis guineensis*) whilst sago is the starchy pulp extracted from the stem of species in the genus *Metroxylone*.

Chusan Palm (*Trachycarpus fortunei*) is one of the hardiest Palms, tolerating the temperate conditions of southern England. It is a Fan Palm and grows to 10m.

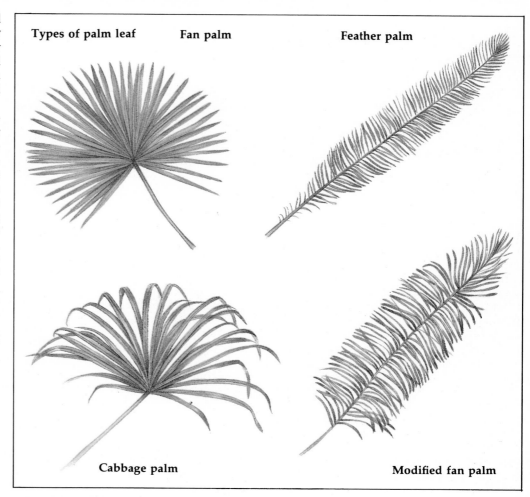

Types of palm leaf **Fan palm** **Feather palm**

Cabbage palm **Modified fan palm**

Above: **farmer wearing a garment of unwoven *Trachycarpus* fibres.**

Left: **Coconut Palms – a characteristic sight of tropical beaches, and an important source of food.**

Bamboos and Tree Ferns

Bamboos (Gramineae) are woody grasses and in many respects behave like grasses. They form shrubs and trees with some tropical species attaining 40m. They are monocotyledons.

Bamboos make all their new growth from the underground rhizome or root system. New shoots or culms are pushed up from below; it is making new growth from the bottom (rather than from the top as in nearly all other plants) that makes grasses so tolerant of mowing and grazing.

The culms of most species grow in two phases. The first phase, lasting about 3 months, is when the culm is made. At this stage it consists of a single cane with numerous nodes, each with a sheath. In the next phase, which in temperate species occurs in the following year, the leaf-bearing shoots grow out from buds at each node. The leaves are evergreen, flat and broad with parallel veins.

Many bamboos are monocarpic – they flower once, usually over a period of a few years, and then die. The curious feature of bamboos is that they have an almost perfect biological clock and all the members of one species, whether cultivated in Europe, Asia, America or New Zealand, will flower at the same time. The period before the species flowers varies: in some it is only twenty-five years but in others it exceeds a century.

Bamboos come as either tuft-forming species, in which the stems arise from one point and the spread of the clump is extremely slow, and rhizomatous species, in which runners or rhizomes are sent out from the clump for several metres, forming culms and new clumps along the way. They require moist conditions and will not tolerate drought and windy sites. In nature they are mainly found in eastern Asia with fewer species in the Americas.

Arundinaria (from America and Asia), *Sasa* (Japan) and *Chusquea* (Central and South America) all have straight round stems. *Sasa* is dwarf and has only a single branch at each node. *Chusquea* has many and differs in floral characters.

Phyllostachys (Japan, China and the Himalayas) and *Shibataea* (E. Asia) have stems which zig-zag and are flattened on each side alternately above the nodes. In *Shibataea* the culms are solid.

Tree Ferns (Dicksoniaceae and Cyatheaceae) are spore-producing plants, and these two small families are the only woody survivors of the ones which formed the coal and oil deposits. They require protection from frost and drying winds, as well as moist and shady conditions; they are restricted in nature to wet tropical and warm temperate regions.

Dicksonia antarctica from Australia is one of the hardiest species. It forms a tree to 10m with a rather palm-like mop of leaves. The trunk is profusely covered with brown hairs. Cyatheaceae is the main family of Tree Ferns, with some species growing to 25m. *Cyathea dealbata* from New Zealand has leaves vividly glaucous below.

Opposite page: **a Punga Tree Fern growing in a New Zealand forest.**

Below: **a stand of bamboo in Malaya**

Places to Visit

Below is a list of some of the world's leading arboreta and botanic gardens.

Australia
Adelaide Botanic Garden, South Australia
Brisbane Botanic Garden, Queensland
Canberra Botanic Garden
Melbourne Botanic Gardens, South Yarra, Victoria
Sydney Botanic Garden, New South Wales
Royal Tasmanian Botanic Gardens, Hobart, Tasmania

Britain
National Pinetum, Bedgebury, Kent
The Botanic Gardens, Bath
University Botanic Garden, Cambridge
Dawyck Arboretum, Stobo, Peebles, Scotland
Royal Botanic Gardens, Kew, Richmond, Surrey
Royal Horticultural Society's Garden, Wisley, Guildford
Wakehurst Place, Sussex
The University of Liverpool Botanic Garden, Ness, Wirral
Westonbirt Arboretum, near Tetbury, Gloucestershire
Borde Hill Gardens, Haywards Heath
The Hillier Arboretum, Romsey, Hants

Canada
Dominion Arboretum, Ottawa
Montreal Botanical Garden, Montreal
Royal Botanic Garden, Hamilton, Ontario

Ireland
Castlewelland Forest Park, County Down, Northern Ireland
National Botanic Gardens, Glasnevin, Dublin

New Zealand
Albert Park, Auckland
Botanic Gardens, Christchurch
Botanic Gardens, Dunedin
Kaingaroa State Forest, Rotorua
Pukeiti Rhododendron Trust, New Plymouth
Waipoua Kauri Forest, Northland
Botanical Gardens, Wellington

United States of America
Arnold Arboretum, Harvard University, Jamaica Plain, Massachusetts
Highland and Durand-Eastman Parks, Rochester, New York
Missouri Botanical Garden, Gray Summit, St. Louis, Missouri
Morton Arboretum, Lisle, Illinois
National Arboretum, Washington, DC
University of Washington Arboretum, Seattle, Washington
University of California Botanic Garden, Berkeley, California
Brooklyn Botanic Garden and Arboretum, Brooklyn, New York
Longwood Gardens, Kennett Square, Pennsylvania
The Holden Arboretum, Mentor, Ohio
The New York Botanic Garden, Bronx, New York
Morris Arboretum, Philadelphia, Pennsylvania

Belgium
Jardin Botanique National de Belgique, Brussels
Arboretum, Kalmthout

Denmark
Arboretet, Hørsholm, Denmark

Finland
Arboretum Mustila, Elimaki, Finland

France
Jardin Botanic de la Ville, Lyon, Rhône
Jardin des plantes de l'Université de Montpellier, Montpellier
Arboretum des Barres et Fructicetum Vilmorinianum, Nugent-sur-Vernisson, Loiret

Japan
Aritaki Arboretum, Ko-shigaya-shi, Saitama-ken

Holland
Wageningen

Sweden
Goteborgs Botaniska Tradgard, Goteborg
The Botanical Garden, Uppsala

Glossary

Angiosperm a plant having its seeds enclosed in an ovary (c.f. gymnosperm).

Anther part of the stamen containing the pollen.

Arboretum collection of trees and woody plants.

Aril outer layer surrounding a seed, usually fleshy; derived from the seed stalk (e.g. Yew).

Bark the external covering of stems, roots and branches.

Bipinnate pinnate with the divisions also pinnate (e.g. *Acacia*).

Calyx sepals of a flower considered as a whole.

Carpel functional unit of the female organ of a flower.

Cellulose the chief constituent of the cell walls of plants, forming an essential part of wood, cotton, paper etc.

Chloroplast cell containing chlorophyll, responsible for photosynthesis.

Cladode a flattened leaf-like branch or stem (e.g. *Phylloclauds*).

Corolla petals of a flower considered as a whole.

Corymb short, broad and more or less flat-topped inflorescence, developing like a raceme (e.g. *Sorbus*).

Cotyledons seed-leaves; the primary or rudimentary leaves of the embryo of plants.

Culm the jointed, usually hollow stem of grasses and bamboos.

Cupule cup-like structure at the base of a fruit, composed of bracts (e.g. the acorn cup of Oaks).

Cuticle transparent film covering the surface of plants.

Dichotomous branching into two parts.

Dicotyledon angiosperm plant with two cotyledons (c.f. monocotyledon).

Drupe fleshy fruit with the seed(s) surrounded by a stony layer (e.g. Cherry).

Elliptic widest at the middle, rounded and narrowed towards each end.

Epiphyte plant which grows upon another but does not obtain nutrients or water from it.

Fascicle a close cluster of flowers or leaves.

Filament part of the stamen, the stalk supporting the anther.

Gametophyte sexually reproducing generation of a plant (c.f. sporophyte).

Gymonsperm plant having its seeds exposed or 'naked', i.e. not enclosed in an ovary.

Heartwood dead wood in the centre of a stem; darker than the sapwood.

Hilum seed-scar; particularly conspicuous on the seeds of Horse Chestnut.

Inflorescence flower cluster, including the stem bearing the flowers and bracts.

Involucre joined bracts, usually surrounding the base of a short dense inflorescence.

Latex the milky sap of certain plants, from which rubber is made.

Legume a dry fruit splitting lengthwise to release its seeds.

Lenticels corky breathing pores on young bark and some fruits (e.g. Whitebeam).

Liana long woody-stemmed climbing plant of tropical forests.

Meristem special groups of actively dividing cells occurring mainly at shoot and root tips.

Monocarpic flowering and fruiting once only and then dying.

Monocotyledon angiosperm plant having only one cotyledon (c.f. dicotyledon).

Monopodial having a single main axis which continues to extend at the apex, giving off lateral branches below.

Mycorrhiza symbiotic association of species of fungus with the roots of trees.

Node point of a stem where a leaf or leaves arise.

Obovate ovate but broadest above the middle.

Operculum rounded cover or lid, particularly of *Eucalyptus* flowers.

Ovary female part of the flower, enclosing the egg(s).

Ovate widest below the middle, rounded towards base, tapered towards tip.

Palmate leaf with more than three veins (simple) or leaflets (compound) arising from the same point.

Panicle inflorescence like a branched raceme.

Parthenogenic of an egg, developing without fertilization.

Pedicel stalk of a flower

Peduncle stalk of an inflorescence, or of a group of flowers within an inflorescence.

Petal one of the parts of a corolla.

Petiole stalk of a leaf.

Phloem cells in the conducting tissue taking the products of photosynthesis around the tree.

Phyllode flattened leaf-like petiole with no blade (as in *Acacia*).

Pinetum collection of conifers.

Pinnate compound leaf with many leaflets or simple leaf with veins arranged either side of a central axis (of stalk or vein).

Pinnule one of the pinnately arranged divisions of a bipinnate leaf.

Pneumatophore breathing root of trees such as mangroves or *Taxodium* which grow in swamps.

Pulvinus outgrowth of a twig from which a leaf or leaflet arises, e.g. *Picea*.

Raceme inflorescence with a central peduncle which continually adds single new (stalked) flowers to the tip; the oldest flowers are therefore at the base.

Radicle the first root to emerge from a seed at germination.

Resin the sap of certain trees, e.g. Pines, used as a source of various products including turpentine.

Rhizome an underground stem, producing both roots below and shoots above.

Rotation period for which plantation trees are grown before felling and replacement.

Samara dry fruit with a wing formed from part of the wall (e.g. *Acer*, *Fraxinus*).

Sapwood the live wood surrounding the dead inner heartwood.

Sepal one of the individual leaves or parts of the calyx of a flower.

Spore cell which becomes free and capable of forming a new plant.

Sporophyte spore or seed reproducing generation of a plant alternating with the gametophyte generation.

Springwood relatively soft wood with large water-conducting vessels, laid down in spring and early summer.

Stamen male reproductive part of a flower, producing pollen and consisting of anther and filament.

Stellate resembling a star.

Stigma pollen-receiving part of the female reproductive organ of a flower.

Stoma (plural stomata) pore, usually in a leaf or stem surface.

Style part of the female reproductive organ of a flower, connecting the stigma to the ovary.

Summerwood wood with thick-walled cells playing a supportive role in the structure of a tree; laid down in summer.

Syncarp an aggregate fruit, e.g. Mulberry.

Tepal petals and sepals together, especially when these are not clearly differentiated (e.g. Magnolia).

Transpiration the emission of water vapour through the stomata on a leaf surface.

Trifoliate having three leaflets.

Umbel inflorescence with all the pedicels or peduncles arising from the same point.

Xylem woody cells in conducting tissue bringing water and nutrients from the roots.

Index